"What does the church have to say when our shame and sadness is unbearable, our loneliness excruciating, and our faith empty? In his amazing book, Michael Card reminds us of the most profound answer–Jesus' presence is all there is. Lament leads us to the hidden face of God."

—SCOTT ROLEY, pastor of Christ Community Church, Franklin, TN;
author of *God's Neighborhood*

"Michael Card is plowing ground that has been fallow for far too long—the field of lament, which has a rich and fertile past in biblical history. His book is a place to plant your tears, a well-watered place where your heart will surely grow."

—KEN GIRE, author of *Moments with the Savior,*
Windows of the Soul, and *The North Face of God*

"When Michael Card sent me a copy of his CD that contained *The Hidden Face of God*, I began playing it over and over and never have stopped. Now the book! Michael is the rare combination of Jesus-glorifying artist/educator/musician/theologian/philosopher/writer. He expresses my heart's deepest longings for which I had never before found words. In his God-given gifting, he encourages me to release every emotion to the Creator and Redeemer of us all."

—DON FINTO, PhD, pastor; director, The Caleb Company

the hidden face of God

Finding the Missing Door to the Father Through Lament

by michael card

NAVPRESS®

BRINGING TRUTH TO LIFE

The Navigators is an international Christian organization. Our mission is to advance the gospel of Jesus and His kingdom into the nations through spiritual generations of laborers living and discipling among the lost. We see a vital movement of the gospel, fueled by prevailing prayer, flowing freely through relational networks and out into the nations where workers for the kingdom are next door to everywhere.

NavPress is the publishing ministry of The Navigators. The mission of NavPress is to reach, disciple, and equip people to know Christ and make Him known by publishing life-related materials that are biblically rooted and culturally relevant. Our vision is to stimulate spiritual transformation through every product we publish.

© 2007 by Michael Card

All rights reserved. No part of this publication may be reproduced in any form without written permission from NavPress, P.O. Box 35001, Colorado Springs, CO 80935.
www.navpress.com

NAVPRESS, BRINGING TRUTH TO LIFE, and the NAVPRESS logo are registered trademarks of NavPress. Absence of ® in connection with marks of NavPress or other parties does not indicate an absence of registration of those marks.

ISBN-10: 157683-669-X
ISBN-13: 978-1-57683-669-9

Cover design by studiogearbox.com
Cover image: Jupiter Images
Creative Team: Don Simpson, Darla Hightower, Arvid Wallen, Kathy Guist

Essay 30 was originally published in *Discipleship Journal* (NavPress).

Unless otherwise identified, all Scripture quotations in this publication are taken from the HOLY BIBLE: NEW INTERNATIONAL VERSION® (NIV®). Copyright © 1973, 1978, 1984 by International Bible Society. Used by permission of Zondervan Publishing House. All rights reserved. Other versions used include: the *Holy Bible, New Living Translation* (NLT), copyright © 1996, 2004. Used by permission of Tyndale House Publishers, Inc., Wheaton, Illinois 60189. All rights reserved; the *New American Standard Bible* (NASB), © The Lockman Foundation 1960, 1962, 1963, 1968, 1971, 1972, 1973, 1975, 1977, 1995; the *English Standard Version* (ESV), copyright © 2001 by Crossway Bibles, a division of Good News Publishers. Used by permission. All rights reserved; and *The Jewish Bible* (JPS), copyright 1985 by the Jewish Publication Society.

Card, Michael, 1957-
  The hidden face of God : finding the missing door to the Father
through lament / by Michael Card.
    p. cm.
  Includes bibliographical references (p.   ).
  ISBN 1-57683-669-X
  1. Hidden God. 2. Grief--Religious aspects--Christianity. 3. Laments.
4. Spiritual life--Christianity. I. Title.
BT180.H54C37 2007
242'.4--dc22
                        2006036710

Printed in the United States of America

1 2 3 4 5 6 7 8 / 11 10 09 08 07

FOR A FREE CATALOG OF NAVPRESS BOOKS & BIBLE STUDIES,
CALL 1-800-366-7788 (USA) OR 1-800-839-4769 (CANADA)

These were my teachers. And there were more,
beloved of face and name, who once bore
the substance of our common ground.
Their eyes, having grieved all grief, were clear.

from "Elegy" by Wendell Berry

Contents

Part Three: A Gathering of the Guilty

Part Four: The Man of Sorrows

Foreword

In the cold wind and mist of an early morning in March 1996, a seven-year-old girl, Jessica Dubroff, along with Jessica's father and a professional pilot, took off in a single-engine Cessna from the municipal airport at Cheyenne, Wyoming. Jessica's purpose: to be the youngest pilot ever to fly across the country. It was a major publicity event followed by all the major news organizations.

Just off the runway, the overweight plane apparently gathered ice on its wings and may have met with wind shear. Whatever the cause, the plane banked left sharply, stalled, and plummeted to the ground, killing all three on board. It was a tragedy that riveted the country's attention. In an interview with *Time* magazine after the crash, Jessica's mother said stoically of those offering her sympathy: "I know what people want. Tears. But I will not do that. Emotion is unnatural. There is something untruthful about it."[1]

Is emotion unnatural? Are tears untruthful? Perhaps Jessica's story — or at least her mother's reaction — seems like an extreme illustration, but we humans have a pattern of denial. "Where was God in Auschwitz?" asked Holocaust survivor and writer Elie Wiesel a few years ago. "Were we unable to hear God's tears because we ourselves have not wept enough?"[2]

Especially in America, we work to control or deny our sorrow. We try to get over it quickly, or we sidestep it altogether by "looking on the good side." Even the music in many churches consists primarily of lighthearted praise choruses, sung to upbeat instrumentation. But does this represent a complete picture of human life? In a sense, it is a denial of a profound underlying reality. The apostle Paul paints a picture of this reality:

> We know that the whole creation has been groaning as in the pains of childbirth right up to the present time. Not only so, but we ourselves,

who have the firstfruits of the Spirit, groan inwardly as we wait eagerly for our adoption as sons, the redemption of our bodies. (Romans 8:22-23)

Even the Spirit of God within us "intercedes for us with groans that words cannot express" (Romans 8:26). We may be certain there is hope in this groaning — for it is a groaning toward God with the vision of a new reality, which Paul represents by the joyous birth of a child following a woman's labor pains.

In the meantime, for people who truly acknowledge the reality of life in a world that bears the effects of sin, we live in a place of weeping. Psalm 84 describes the pilgrims who traveled up to Jerusalem for the great festivals as passing through the "valley of weeping." Weeping was considered a fundamental element of our pilgrimage through this fallen world.

But God listens to this weeping. The great mercy of God in setting His people free was a response to enslaved and oppressed Israel's anguished tears (Exodus 3:7). Later, captive and forlorn Israel's exile was drenched in tears (Psalm 137:1). And the disciples heard the tears of God Himself, for the days of Jesus' life on earth were characterized by "loud cries and tears" (Hebrews 5:7).

My dear friend, Mike Card, has spent many years immersed in a profound awareness of creation's groaning. He has much to teach us all. Mike has visited places and listened to people around the world where that groaning is a daily, grinding reality. But he has also immersed himself in the Bible's message of the lamentation of God's people, for the Bible gives us the right patterns to begin to respond to sin and suffering — our own and that of the rest of the world.

Mike seeks the engagement of God's people today in what he rightly calls "the lost language of lament." He says we have been missing something important in our relating to God. Biblical faith is a comprehensive view of reality. We have not been touched to our depths if we have bypassed the Bible's teaching on lament. And it is this longing, this groaning, these anguished tears that move the heart of God for the salvation of the world.

If the cries and tears of Jesus were able to reach the ears of "the one who could save him from death," then we owe our own lives to Jesus' tears. Lament is a powerful gift of God to human beings. We need to learn how to use it. Listen to Mike Card as he wisely and engagingly teaches us this lost language.

— Don Simpson

Introduction: The Missing Door

On a glorious July morning, a shabbily dressed thirty-seven-year-old man stepped outside the door of his rented room, a battered hat pulled down low over his shock of thick, red hair. Slung over his shoulder was a rucksack containing paints and brushes as well as the palette knife he was occasionally known to use instead of a brush, applying the paint as thick as frosting. He grasped a folded easel in his right hand, a blank canvas comfortably tucked under his left arm. His intention that morning was to paint the sweep of the French countryside, a field of golden, ripening wheat just north of town.

Art had come to dominate his heart and mind in the past ten years. He had originally tried to follow in the footsteps of his father and become a pastor, but he had repeatedly failed his theological entrance exams. Undeterred by this academic failure, he attempted to follow a more missional call and serve the poorest of the poor. For three long, cold months he had ministered in a small coal mining town in Belgium. There, like Frances of Assisi, he sought to literally follow the call of Jesus, giving away all his possessions. One after another, his paychecks vanished into the bottomless need of the miners and their families. So completely did he reflect the sacrificial simplicity of Jesus that he became known as "the Christ of the coal mines."

But those in the church who had authority over him did not feel this extravagance was appropriate, and he was eventually dismissed. It was a failure that hounded him for the rest of his life.

During the ensuing decade, he realized that it was not to the pulpit he was called, but to painting. It became his goal to "bring consolation to humanity through art." No one ever worked harder in obedience to such a call. In the volumes of his letters (1,670 pages of them!) to his brother Theo, he obsessed about the guilt that hounded him for not getting his "work" done, for not finishing more paintings. The two of them had grown up in a church tradition where faith demanded doing more, not loving more.

In the weeks before that glorious July morning, this "works righteousness" ethic seemed to finally be working for him. His troubled mind seemed to clear somewhat. His themes returned to more "spiritual" subjects. He had even lately painted a picture of a church.

At last he reached the field that was to be his subject for the morning. He unfolded his easel, carefully placing the canvas upon it. He began to work for a brief moment, but suddenly he reached into his pocket and withdrew a small-caliber revolver, pointed the barrel at his chest, and pulled the trigger. Seemingly unsuccessful, even in his own suicide, he limped home and died a few days later. His name was Vincent van Gogh.

It could reasonably be claimed that no one in his time had a more gifted "eye." His remarkable, often disturbing, sense of line and color produced paintings the like of which had never been seen. He portrayed flowers in sizzling colors that, though perhaps not botanically correct, provide the viewer with the true impression, almost the fragrance of the things themselves. His swirling stars are not strictly speaking representative pictures as much as invitations to see and experience the stars through the remarkable gift of his eye. But of all that Vincent's imagination could see and translate into charcoal and paint, the one thing he needed most to see he was never able to fully perceive.

That difficult mission trip to the Belgian coal mines resulted in his becoming estranged from the church he longed to serve. As with so many others, Vincent's separation from the church established a rift between himself and Christ as well. Though he refers to suicide more than once in his vast correspondence with his brother Theo, especially during the last few months of his life, he rarely mentions Christ. All along he keeps up the constant din of "working harder," "doing more," and "finishing my work." Blinded by the demands of the present moment, by the litany of tasks that were never "done," he had ceased working on the one thing that mattered most — his relationship with Christ.

One of Vincent's last paintings from what is known as the final "revival period," is the church at Auver. It is immediately recognizable as a "van Gogh," with the mass of the gray building framed by a swirling yellow footpath. Above, the deeply blue sky seems almost angry. On one side, a solitary peasant woman has taken the right fork of the path around the church. She is little more than a few brush strokes.

What many art critics have commented on is not the swimming colors but the ominous lack of a doorway leading into the church. Vincent painted a church that no one could get into. Having tried all his life to work hard enough to "get in," it appears that he could not imagine, in this last image of the church, a door that might allow him, with his

enormous load of pain, to enter in. (Critics of this interpretation counter that from the point of view of the painting, the door is simply on the other side of the building. Still, this is the perspective that Vincent chose.) Together with the scarcity of references to Jesus in his last letters, the absence of the door in the painting reveals his most fundamental fear: that there is no way into the church and, even more agonizing, that there is no One waiting on the other side of the missing door.

Though Vincent had spoken repeatedly in the letters of his depression, his struggle with melancholy, his remorse, what he refers to as "an undercurrent of vague sadness," interestingly there is hardly a single mention of tears, his own or anyone else's. (His landlady did report once that she had heard him weeping alone in his room.) He wrote of a guilty desire to "learn to suffer without complaint." His final self-portraits lend credence to this suppression. If you look closely at Vincent's eyes, it is hard to imagine a single tear ever falling from them. They reveal instead a silent simmering confusion. Perhaps suffering without complaint, keeping the tears of his emotional pain under control, was simply another one of those things Vincent was forever "working on."

"La tristesse durera toujours"

It has been said time and again, "there will never be another van Gogh," and in one sense this is perfectly true. But from another point of view, it might also be that there have never been so many "Vincents" in our time—men and women who find themselves standing outside a church with no door, tormented by the possibility that no one could be waiting inside for them. According to their fragmented vision, the only possible solution is to work harder, get busy, and take control. If their portraits could be painted, they too would reveal eyes that were incapable of weeping their own tears much less anyone else's. The most we could hope to see spattered across a thousand canvases are expressions of a hollow happiness, a self-manufactured stoicism, a simpering, "I'm OK, you're OK." Once there is no longer any hope for the One who became acquainted with their grief, then there is no conceivable reason to weep with those who weep, or to even weep for themselves. The door is missing. There is no way in and no One inside.

In an upstairs room of the Ravoux Inn, on July 27, 1890, two days after his suicide attempt, Vincent van Gogh died of his self-inflicted wound. His brother Theo, who was by his side, reported that the last words he whispered were, *"La tristesse durera toujours,"* "the sadness will last forever." It is the inescapable conclusion of anyone who looks honestly at the fallenness of the world but fails to perceive that there is a door and that Someone is waiting on the other side. They are all linked—the missing door, the empty church, and the absent tears. I have come to believe and trust and hope that tears of lament are the missing door, the way into an experience with a God whose depth of compassion we have never imagined.

The following pages represent the continuation of a journey of lament that began with *A Sacred Sorrow*. In that book I sought to lay a foundation for understanding lament through the lives of Job, David, Jeremiah, and Jesus. Now I would like to invite you to travel further along this difficult path with me, to see the safe sanctuary that is lament, to understand that we are called to weep with the poor and the prisoner, that we should ask for the gift of grieving for our own sins and, finally, that we should recognize in a fresh way all that it means to call Jesus the "Man of Sorrows."

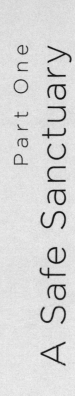

Part One

A Safe Sanctuary

1 | Awakening the God Who Never Sleeps

Awaken, oh my God.
PSALM 7:6

The first, faltering steps in the direction of thinking biblically about God invariably lead us to stumble over paradox. The Bible seems to be saying two mutually exclusive things at the same time: for example, that Jesus is fully man and at the same time fully God. Some people make light of this clash of contraries. "Don't worry about understanding it," they say. "You just need more faith." Others insist that "God is reasonable," and so they conclude that the biblical God must be rejected for their more reasonable god. The first group doesn't take the problem of paradox seriously enough. The second group doesn't take God seriously enough. Both groups are wrong and both groups are right. (Ha! A paradox!)

Yes, we do need more faith to survive the scandal of the paradoxical God. But this dilemma is no small thing to simply be "gotten over." More faith won't fix the problem. The second group is also right: it is a wall that is impossible to scale. But the same God who commands centenarians to make babies consistently calls upon us to do the impossible as well (Genesis 17:17).

The Father knows our struggle with paradox. He revealed this awareness once in a pronouncement to Isaiah that began with God paradoxically urging the people to come and buy wine and milk, though they have no money. Later he whispered to Isaiah: "My thoughts are not your thoughts, neither are your ways my ways" (55:8).

The Father does not think like us, and so neither does He do things the way we would do them. If we could think infinite thoughts, we would not be people. If He did things the decidedly imperfect way we do, He would not be God.

Imagine we were at the Superdome and I asked you to go outside and put your arms around the building. Supposing you were loony enough to try, you would stretch one arm in one direction and reach as far as you could with the other arm the opposite way. If your arms were long enough, they would meet on the opposite side. You would have "grasped" the Superdome.

The same is true whenever we try to comprehend God. We stretch our minds in one direction and say *Jesus is fully man*. Then we reach out with our imaginations in the other direction and say *He is God*. If our minds were big enough, they would meet on the other side of the truth. As it is, however, we are left making two seemingly contradictory statements, often appearing no less loony than the person trying to hug the Superdome.

One such paradox that makes its way into many biblical laments involves the sleeping God. In Psalm 121:4, the unnamed musician says that, "he who watches over Israel will neither slumber nor sleep." It is supposed to be a lyric of comfort. It is good to know, after all, that the One who is watching over you is not ever going to fall asleep on the job (compare Psalm 4:8).

But what are we to make of those paradoxical moments when this God who never slumbers appears to be asleep, when we are crying out for the help only He can provide and the only response seems to be a kind of holy snoring from the other side of heaven? When we are caught in the midst of a storm, how are we supposed to awaken someone who never sleeps? (Job 19:7; 30:20). How do we call out so the Lord will rise up, as though waking from sleep? (Psalm 44:23).

Early in the ministry of Jesus, He and His disciples were caught in the middle of a huge, demonic storm on the Sea of Galilee. The Gospels describe it as a "seismos," an enormous shaking. Though commentaries frequently explain the storm in terms of the normal meteorological patterns in and around Galilee, the truth is the disciples had never seen a storm like this before. All together in one small boat, it was Satan's chance to wipe them all out in one blow.

But Jesus, the Son of God, was asleep in the midst of the tempest. If it had been one of their customarily calm crossings of the lake, the Twelve might have been able to understand. But the boat is about to sink! "How," they say to themselves, "could he possibly be asleep in the midst of a storm like this? Doesn't he care about us?"

Mark, who tells the story from Peter's perspective, says the disciples castigated Jesus. "Don't you care if we drown?" they scream above the storm.

Jesus lifts His head from the little, rough pillow that was normally used by the man who steered the boat, wipes the sleep from His eyes, and rebukes the storm. "Be muzzled!" He says. They are the same words He speaks when He casts out demons. With two words the attack disappears completely. Turning to the Twelve, perhaps with a yawn lingering on His lips, He says, "Where is your faith?"

Trapped in the middle of a storm on a boat that is sinking. All the while, the One who could calm the storm with a word, sleeps blissfully unaware. Sound familiar? Is this your life? It frequently is mine.

Just when He calls us into relationship, just when we "get into His boat," as it were, the storm descends on us. We are called to follow the Way, and yet we seem always to get lost, to lose Him.

This is not the time to try harder. This is not the moment to strain to manufacture more faith. It is the occasion to cry louder to the One, who though He may seem asleep, is most significantly still present with us in the boat. He is there to be awakened by our cries. He is moved to act by our tears. If you think about it, this is the very first lesson we learned as infants—a persistent cry will bring help.

The story of the storm on the sea is more than a parable. It is more than a lived-out example of being saved, not from but *through* the tempest that would destroy our lives. It is all that and much more. It is a story that prophetically appears in the Psalms as well. Besides the detailed description of the death of Jesus, it is the only other story in the Gospels that makes such a prophetic appearance in the Psalter.

In Psalm 107, a song that celebrates the *hesed* (loving kindness) of the God who makes provision for those in the wilderness, for those in tears, for those in misery and chains—the God who humbles those who rebel against Him—we find an account of the same storm we read about in the Gospels.

In verse 23, those who "went out on the sea in ships," who make their living as fishermen, are promised that they will see His wonders. What follows is an emotional pretelling of what the Gospels only provide as a newspaper account. In verse 28 they cry out to the One who can save them, and the seas are "hushed."

This simple, trusting cry comes from the lips of those of us who are learning that our last hope has always been our only hope — this cry that awakens the God who never sleeps.

For Discussion

1. What other parallels can we draw from the incident of Jesus asleep in the boat? How does His question, "Don't you have any faith?" apply to us when we cry out for God to wake up?

2. Which is worse, to stop believing in God, or to feel as though for the moment He has turned His face away? (Don't be too quick to come to a conclusion.)

For Meditation

1. What would God hope to accomplish by "withdrawing His presence"?

2. Consider how fundamental is that first lesson that a persistent cry will awaken someone to help us. It is placed in us as a matter of survival.

2 | Come Lift Up Your Sorrows

You do not delight in sacrifice, or I would bring it;
you do not take pleasure in burnt offerings.
PSALM 51:16

If anyone seemed to have something to offer God, it was David. He was successful in battle, a real "winner." He had established his own kingdom. He was a gifted musician and lyricist. He was able, most of the time, to access the deeper recesses of his soul and find there the words and images that you and I are still using to communicate with God all these centuries later. David simply had it all. But he wanted more.

When he saw Uriah's wife, Bathsheba, bathing on the rooftop, completing the process of purification from her menstrual uncleanness, David decided he must have her for himself. In the process, he dragged both Bathsheba and himself down into a place infinitely more unclean. Upon discovering that his sexual sin had resulted in Bathsheba becoming pregnant, David sought to cover the whole business up by means of an elaborate deception which ended in the death of Uriah. Lust, rape, treachery, and finally murder.

When his deception of Bathsheba's noble Hittite husband failed, David committed what is perhaps the most cold-blooded act of the whole sordid story. He gave Uriah a dispatch to deliver to Joab, his commanding officer; a letter containing the plot for his own destruction. No Hollywood writer could conceive a more treacherous story, nor a more despicable character than David, the Lord's beloved.

Despite his creative genius, David possessed a fundamental sightless stupidity we all share in common: the foolishness of trying to hide something from Someone who is omniscient. David's willful blindness could only be healed by the painful opening of his eyes.

That task was given to Nathan. The simple parable of the poor man and his lamb was all it took to bait the hook. David bit hard, but hardly struggled once he knew he had been caught. "I have sinned against the LORD," he whispered (2 Samuel 12:13).

But before David had time to take a breath, Nathan pronounced that he was forgiven. He would not experience the death his sin deserved, but the innocent, nameless child that was the result of David's adultery eventually would. I believe it may very well have been during the seven days David pleaded with God to spare the little boy's life that he wrote Psalm 51, his greatest lament of contrition. As he pleaded for God to wash, cleanse, and create a clean heart in him, I wonder just where the little boy was in his imagination. I wonder if he begged to be forgiven, having already been told by Nathan that he was, in hopes that some of that forgiveness would overflow and find its way to his unnamed, week-old son.

In verse 16, David's lament makes a turn. I wonder if it coincides with his discovery that the innocent newborn had finally died (2 Samuel 12:18). Something breaks deep inside his soul, or perhaps something finally opens — his eyes or perhaps a door that had been long closed. In that moment, David realizes two important facts about his condition before God: First, he has forfeited everything and has nothing left to give; second, all he has left, a broken spirit and a contrite heart, is all God ever wanted.

And so the musician, who in his time had lifted up the most moving, glorious, and worshipful songs of praise the world has ever heard, lifts up the bloody, fragmented pieces of what used to be his heart. He takes a deep breath, exhaling his guilt and the burden of his sin and breathes in the Spirit he had begged that God would never take from him. The greatest worshiper of all time enacts the most profound moment of worship . . . alone and in tears. In his complete brokenness he trusts and hopes and believes that this sacrifice of contrition and brokenness will be acceptable.

What about you?

For Discussion

1. There is no word of anger on God's part toward David. Did this shape David's response in Psalm 51?

2. Zechariah sings that Jesus' coming would mean that now we can serve God without fear (Luke 1:74). Discuss the implications of this truth in light of David's realization in Psalm 51.

For Meditation

1. Take a moment to consider, in the light of Psalm 51:17, what your personal offerings might be, the content of your own contrite spirit, the sorrow of your heart.

2. Consider just how God uses the parable of our lives to convict and convince of sin the way he used Nathan's parable (2 Samuel 12).

3 | Two Inescapable Realities

Yet man is born to trouble as surely as sparks fly upward.
JOB 5:7

I must admit, I don't like agreeing with Eliphaz, one of Job's friends whom God condemned for error (Job 42:7). But the above statement is undeniable. More than that, it is inescapable.

Moses agreed. In the only psalm we have from him, a lament, Moses states that our lives are but trouble and sorrow, and we finish them with a moan (Psalm 90:9-10). Even the most hardened atheist would agree that this world is not the way it is supposed to be. Suffering and disease, by their very nature, are simply out of place in this world. They do not belong here, which makes their dominance all the more disturbing. Something within tells us they are out of place. The only reason is that we were not created for this. There is no corner of the world where suffering does not reign, whether it is the world of swollen, starving, HIV-infected Africa or lonely, neurotic, morbidly obese America. The world is fallen, impregnated by inescapable suffering. This is the first of two given realities we cannot escape.

The second is God Himself (Genesis 1:1 — Revelation 22:21). For those who believe, His hand is even more pervasive, more evident, more universal than suffering. Even the most hardened agnostic, sensing the impending deathblow of the lion, the crashing of the tsunami, or the crushing pain of the coronary, cries out to Someone when the moment is upon him. Even as all mankind experiences suffering, so too we are all haunted by the Other whom some of us believe we know and others will deny with their last breath. He is here.

David, in Psalm 139, celebrates God's inescapability. There is no place we can hide from God, sings the psalmist. He is before and behind, up in heaven and down in the depths, on the far side of the sea. If we are swallowed up in darkness, behold, sings David, He is there. His reality is inescapable.

Suffering and God. Superficially, they seem mutually exclusive, like darkness and light, matter and antimatter. What does one have to do with the other? How and at what point could they possibly meet? What would be the result if they did?

The place where these two inescapable realities meet is in lament. Here, the suffering of man for God embraces the suffering of God for man. Here we surrender our running from the inescapability of suffering and raise the white flag to the ever-present One whom David celebrated. Job, overwhelmed by the ordeal, cried out, "I recant and relent; being but dust and ashes" (42:6, JPS). The stumbling, exhausted, world-weary place where suffering and God meet is lament.

What takes place in that meeting is as miraculous as it is unexpected. The two do not simply destroy one another, as matter and antimatter would. Nor does one simply overcome the other and win the battle. No, the One who is Light and Life enters into the suffering and confusion of the other, into his or her darkness and death. God defeats suffering by surrendering Himself to it. He triumphs through exhausting Himself against it, by drinking the cup dry. The miracle that takes place is salvation! The God from whom we cannot escape uses inescapable suffering to save the world that has been in headlong flight from Him ever since the Fall.

The miracle has taken place, once and for all, on a cosmic level at the Cross of Jesus. And yet, the miracle occurs again and again at the level of each individual soul whenever we lament and make a place for our unbearable suffering to come together with the inescapable God.

For Discussion

1. How do the world's religions deal with the problem of suffering?
2. Discuss the implications of the truth that God uses suffering and doesn't simply exist to put an end to it (John 9:1-3; 11:4).

For Meditation

1. Meditate on the concept of all suffering coming together with the fullness of God on the cross.

2. In the presence of suffering, can you see that a complaining lament is still an act of faith?

4 | Older Than the Rain

For the LORD had not yet sent rain on the earth . . . but a mist came up
from the earth and watered the whole surface of the ground.

GENESIS 2:5-6

The light and the air of Eden must have been indescribably different before our first ancestors committed the sin that any one of us would have committed. What the world was like before the Fall is beyond our imaginations. We have no adjectives to describe it, and even if we did, our minds could not take it in. We have only known this fallen world. In order to understand Eden, the Fall would have to be undone in our minds and imaginations.

We do possess one comprehensible adjective that describes the unfallen world: misty. Genesis 2:5 gives us a tantalizing peek into the unfallen garden. Though it must have been extraordinarily lush and green, oddly there was no rain. Instead, God watered the garden by means of a mysterious mist that arose from the earth. Whatever else we cannot describe or imagine about Eden, we can say this: It was misty there.

The first rain did not actually fall until Genesis chapter 6 and the flood of Noah. Then it was as if the whole of creation, from the foundations of the earth to the sky, wept a flood of raindrops. Perhaps this was a result of the fact that God Himself was lamenting, deeply sorry that He had made man (Genesis 6:6). Lament became the language of all creation (Romans 8:22).

Though there is no specific word of them weeping, when Adam and Eve stumbled out of the garden, having heard God's pronouncement of pain and sorrow for them both (Genesis 3:16-19), it is impossible to imagine them dry-eyed. (Note: Certainly, they were created with tear ducts, but these appear to exist primarily to keep the eyes lubricated with tears.) Weeping is an older and more fundamental part of life on earth than the falling rain. There were teardrops before there were raindrops.

Human tears are older than the rain.

If you think about it, teardrops and raindrops have a lot in common. The rain occurs when the clouds become oversaturated, usually in association with a change in pressure in the atmosphere. Tears occur when our souls become oversaturated with pain or joy. Somewhere inwardly, a pressure builds up, which is only released when our tears start to flow. Even as the ground is watered and nourished by the drops of rain, so it is time for us to wake up to the nourishment and healing power of tears. Those small salty drops that burn our eyes are as fundamental to life as food and air. They are a mystery that cannot be explained away.

Most of us do our best to hide our tears. We try to hold back the pressure when we sense it building in our hearts. We mistakenly believe that if we can control our tears then we can control the pain.

Jesus seems never to have done this. He is so exquisitely tuned to His soul that whenever suffering appeared, His own or anyone else's, Jesus wept. His tears come freely when He arrives on the scene of the death of His close friend Lazarus. This was not a weakness but one of His greatest strengths.

He weeps tears of compassion when He sees Mary's tears and confusion (John 11:35).

He weeps when He sees Jerusalem, knowing the extent of the destruction that is just around the corner (Luke 19:41).

He weeps for sorrow in the garden, confessing to His disciples that the sorrow is about to kill Him (Mark 14:34).

Jesus was no stranger to the mystery of tears. He never once hid his face when it was wet with them. If He was to be fully human, then tears had to be a fundamental part of the incarnate experience for Him. Like you and me, the first sound Jesus made to show that He was alive was the sound of weeping.

And so, from Jesus we learn that in order for us to become complete, to become fully human, we must take tears more seriously. We must understand that following Jesus, the Man of Sorrows, will mean more tears for us, not less. Perhaps we should be reminded of all this every time we sense the pressure changing and experience the "tears of the sky," realizing all along that our own tears are older and more fundamental.

For Discussion

1. What is lost when a people, a church, or a denomination denies the primary place of tears?

2. How is what we believe about the legacy of lament tied to our hope that lament will someday come to an end? (Revelation 21:4).

For Meditation

1. Think back to your earliest memory of tears. Now recall the last time you wept. How are those two moments connected?

2. Spend some time thinking about tears as a bridge between sorrow and joy.

5 | The God Who Takes Everything Away

Son of man, . . . I am about to take away from you the delight of your eyes.

Ezekiel's ministry began with a curious consumption — a meal of lament. When he was first called by God to speak to His "rebellious people" who were in exile in Babylon, the Lord laid out a scroll before this priest who was to become a prophet. When Ezekiel looked at the scroll, he discovered that written on both sides were "words of lament and mourning and woe" (2:10). It was an ominous way for a ministry to begin.

When he was commanded to eat the scroll upon which such bitter words had been inscribed, he was surprised to discover that it tasted as sweet as honey. It was only his first step into a world where everything would be radically reversed, where the wisdom of God would be demonstrated through Ezekiel's foolish prophetic activities — lying on the ground bound and naked, make-believe journeys, digging holes through walls. Even in the wildest of his wild dreams, Ezekiel could not have imagined the reversal that was to come.

It was the first time God had ever referred to him directly by name. Usually he was called by the circumlocution "son of man," or in some translations simply "human." It would be his last oracle against Judah, the conclusion of the first great block of prophecies of the one who had been called to the exilic community in Babylon. When the people would gather for prayer by one of the canals of the Euphrates River known as Kebar, the prophet would appear to pronounce or denounce or to act out one of his difficult messages from the Lord. This final word would be the most difficult for them all, especially Ezekiel.

To get a glimpse into the Jewish hearts of his listeners, we need to understand that their security and confidence was based on a simple triad: Land, King, and Temple. As a result of the exile, they had effectively lost the land and their king. All they had left, though they were physically separated from it by more than six hundred miles, was the Temple. "The Place," they called it, *ha makom*, the center of the Universe. It was their one remaining source of hope, pride, and confidence. If God's house is still there in Jerusalem, perhaps someday soon He will return to inhabit it and save the people, His "treasured possession." Though the community struggled theologically with the defeat of their king (and their God) and their expulsion from the land of promise to Babylon, the fact that the Temple, the house of their God, still remained, represented literally their last hope.

We know absolutely nothing about her, except that she was his wife, the "delight of his eyes." We do not know her name or what tribe she was from. It would be helpful to know what her attitude was toward her husband's difficult calling, but there is not a single word of it. We are left to assume that the marriage was a solid one — after all, she was the light of his life.

In chapter 24, the word comes to Ezekiel: His wife's life will be taken and Ezekiel is to show no signs of mourning, not a single tear. That morning the prophet preached the message, and in the evening, his beloved died. It was August 14, 586 BC. At the same instant, some six hundred miles away in Jerusalem, the Temple was in flames.

As best he could, Ezekiel was obedient to the torturous command. There is hardly an image more troubling than that of a man standing beside the grave of his wife. But when it is seen that that same man has no tears in his eyes, the image becomes deeply disturbing. Something has gone terribly wrong.

The people immediately recognize that this is yet another example of Ezekiel's prophetic activity. They understand that he has become a sign. Ezekiel would incarnate their wordless suffering. He would be the portent of the one who had the last thing that meant anything to him violently taken away. He is the tearless sign.

In time, the exiles received word that their last reason for hope, the

Temple, no longer existed. It had been destroyed along with their children who had been left behind in the Holy City. Ezekiel's prophecy had come true. The Temple of Solomon, the delight of their eyes, was utterly destroyed by Nebuchadnezzar. But, according to God's command, there will be no tears for the Temple.

Not until now — with the last source of their security gone — would they be ready to weep in earnest for what they should have been lamenting from the start: their sin.

Some have concluded that the heart of this message is still a mystery. There is no simple answer that squeezes the story dry. But woven into the inscrutability of the story is a truth so fundamental and dark that it is even harder to put into words. It is as dark as the cloud of unknowing that surrounds God. The truth of the story of the unwept Temple is this: The Lord is a God who takes everything away.

Abram was called to leave. Job lost everything a man can lose. Jesus let go and gave up all, and calls us unequivocally to do the same, or else we cannot be His disciples. Only when we can tearlessly leave our last hope, can we receive the hope that is in Him.

He will take away what you perceive as your last hope, whether it is your place (land), your authority (king), or whatever might be the "delight of your eyes" (Temple). He will drive you to the wilderness where all your hopes will die. Only there can a new hope be born.

To lament is to mourn the death of your last hope, to cry out, to complain, to wrestle with the One who promises to be your only hope.

For Discussion

1. Discuss the differing outcomes of running away from your grief versus redemptively entering into it.

2. Compare a global tragedy to a small personal one. Is there a scale to suffering?

For Meditation

1. Imagine the person you love most in the world being taken away. Try to be honest and imagine what your response to God might be.

2. Now put yourself in Ezekiel's place and consider the impact on your relationship with the Lord who commands you not to weep.

6 | An Honest Hopelessness

A voice is heard in Ramah,
weeping and great mourning,
Rachel weeping for her children
and refusing to be comforted,
because they are no more.

MATTHEW 2:18

The first time we meet her in the Bible (Genesis 29:6), she is a young and beautiful shepherdess. Her face is flush from running alongside her father's sheep. She has led the flock there to be watered at the well. She is one of Laban's two daughters — the prettier one. (Her sister, Leah, was said to have "weak" eyes.)

Jacob, the dreamer, is fresh from his experience at Bethel, where he saw a ladder coming down from heaven and angels ascending and descending upon it. But when he sees Rachel for the first time, he doesn't know if he's dreaming or not.

Wide-eyed, Jacob rolls the stone from the mouth of the well, leans forward, kisses her sun-kissed cheek, and breaks down in tears. At this moment of her life, she is as beautiful as she will ever be. Her eyes are dark and clear, and at this point she cannot see all the barren years that lie before her like an expanse of desert. Neither can she imagine how that wilderness will end with the birth of Joseph. For now she is the stunning shepherdess, blushing at just having been kissed by a stranger.

The last time we see Rachel, her image could not be more different. She is no longer the vivacious young girl but a desolate, abandoned woman consumed by inconsolable grief. The dark, almond eyes have swollen shut from weeping as she collapses by the road to Ramah, just outside Jerusalem. In his own tear-filled eyes, Jeremiah prophetically sees her, a living symbol of the suffering of the northern tribes being led away into captivity. Her kinsmen are being herded north, like sheep, to Babylon, never to return. Whenever someone tries to console her, she shrinks away. Rachel "refuses to be comforted."

Jeremiah, who knew more about grief than anyone else in the Old Testament, recognized this disturbing, final stage of lament. More than once he had seen the kind of suffering that desperately reached out for comfort, whether it could be found or not. He had seen others who eventually became numb to the pain, who had suffered so long they had forgotten what it was like to be comforted. But by far the worst was this final stage, where the sufferer would violently drive away any attempt at being comforted. These inconsolable ones were the most desolate. They had come to the darkest place: the realization that there was no comfort for their suffering. It simply no longer existed.

Jeremiah heard the echo of such sobs six hundred years distant, still coming from the direction of Ramah, near Bethlehem. It was the screams of Rachel's descendents, crying the same inconsolable cry. Herod had slaughtered every innocent male infant in an attempt to murder the new King of the Jews. It reverberated back six centuries and fell upon the prophet's ear.

The next time you witness suffering of this magnitude, whether it's on television or perhaps closer to home, take a moment and listen more intently. Amid all the contrapuntal strains of grief, listen for a single, unexpected note: honesty.

Those who are lost in this wilderness of grief, most especially at the loss of a child, have come to know that there is no comfort for what they are experiencing, no morning at the end of this long dark night. Theirs is an honest hopelessness that sees with a disturbing clarity through their tears that there is no hope. It simply does not exist . . . anywhere. Neither is there the seed of the hope that it ever will exist.

At this darkest stage — in order for comfort to exist — it must be created out of the nothingness that smothers the sufferer. Comfort *ex nihilo*, which is to say, a comfort that can only come from the God who alone can create something out of nothing.

Jesus whispered to Jairus, who has just lost his own little girl, "Don't be afraid, just believe." He calmly told the inconsolable Mary, "Your brother will rise again." And then He proceeded to create life out of the chaos of death and comfort from the nothingness of their despair.

Hope where even the possibility of hope does not exist. Comfort for those who are comfortless. For those who, in honest hopelessness, refuse to be comforted with the pale distractions of this world, the pointless poems, the pious slogans, or the next cure, He comes, the Word of Comfort — for "comforter" is one of His names (John 14:16).

For Discussion
1. How does God use the perspective of hopelessness?
2. Is giving up on any other hope altogether the right thing in a fallen world? The sensible thing?

For Meditation
1. As long as any other source of hope exists, besides the hope of the Comforter, can either true hope or comfort be found?
2. Think back to the most painful experience of your life. When hope came at last, what form did it take? Were there any experiences of false hope before the real thing finally arrived? Are you still waiting for it to come?

7 | Wisdom, Sorrow, and *Hesed*

For with much wisdom comes much sorrow;
the more knowledge, the more grief.

ECCLESIASTES 1:18

If Ecclesiastes is any indication, Solomon was a spent force at the end of his life. I can see him reclining on his favorite carved ivory couch, brooding in his "Palace of the Forest of Lebanon," so called because either a forest of trees was cut down to build it or the rows upon rows of cedar columns inside looked like a forest (1 Kings 7:2-12). He occasionally takes a sip from a golden goblet. Everything in his house was made of gold, because he thought silver had little or no value (1 Kings 10:21). The wine has been brought from Egypt. It is the favorite vintage of the daughter of Pharaoh, the most recent addition to his overcrowded harem. He literally has more of everything than anyone else in the world — more wealth, more power, more wives, more respect, more fame, and above all, more wisdom.

When he was still a boy, Solomon, who might have asked God for anything, had asked for wisdom (1 Kings 3:3-9). God responded by granting wisdom as well as all the wealth he might have asked for. But of all the untold, incalculable riches the Father lavished on the young king there was one, the most precious of all, that Solomon did not seem to treasure. Perhaps it was because he knew this most priceless gift was offered to everyone.

As he was formulating his request for wisdom, he twice mentioned the loving-kindness (*hesed*) that had been the defining characteristic of the relationship between his father, David, and the Lord. Solomon must have recognized some value in it, but in the end that is not what he asked for. So God gladly gave the young king the wisdom for which he asked plus the wealth for which he had not asked. And there, sadly, Solomon seems to have remained, demonstrating the fact that no one ever asks God for the one thing they need the most.

The old man shifts from one elbow to the other, absentmindedly knocking to the ground a scroll. It unrolls across the polished cedar floor. It is a lengthy work on the topic of wisdom, and he feels it is almost complete, though he has made only one sad conclusion in the entire work. He has spent his celebrated life knowing all the answers, and in the end for him it all boils down to one word, "meaningless." Everything you and I could dream of possessing, he owns. Anything we could imagine doing, he has done. And it means nothing. Perhaps this is because he has never really wanted, in all his misdirected desires, the one thing that we all can possess.

In Ecclesiastes the word *hesed* does not appear a single time! It is a monologue full of proverbial wisdom. Though it plumbs the depth of emotional darkness, there is *not a single word of lament*. Solomon speaks frequently about God in the course of the book. But not once does he speak *to* God. Perhaps that is why he remains in his own personal gloom. Though Ecclesiastes contains the words of the wisest of men, even at the end of his life with God, he had not begun his journey to God.

The lesson of Solomon's life, and of his book, is not that wisdom is somehow bad, nor even that worldly wealth is meaningless. The lesson is that without *hesed* nothing can be good. Nothing has any real meaning apart from a relationship with God on His gracious terms.

Like Job, Solomon learned the hard way (which unfortunately is the only way to learn) that talking about God and talking to God are two completely different things. The wisest man who ever lived, the person who could utter the smartest things about God, can come to the end of a blessed life and find only meaninglessness. While the fool, who spends his years only stuttering and stammering to God, can come to the end of the painful journey of his life and find God waiting for him there.

The sated sage slowly rises from his ivory bed and shuffles down the long colonnaded corridor, floored in the finest polished marble, in the direction of the harem. At the last moment he turns back in the direction of the "Hall of

Justice," where his golden throne sits atop a staircase flanked by twelve lions. He knows that in the afternoon no one will be there. He slowly climbs the six steps, slumps into the golden chair, and spends the remainder of the evening asking himself what it was that he missed.

For Discussion

1. Make a list of six or eight wealthy and powerful people in the world, living or dead. One by one, examine together the outcome of their lives.

2. How many died in despair?

For Meditation

1. Search deep inside and honestly ask yourself if a God of *hesed* is what you really want.

2. How does the way you relate to Him change once you begin to realize this fundamental dimension (*hesed*) of His character?

8 | Through the Wilderness

That they may worship Me in the wilderness

Exodus 7:16, JPS

Outlines, word studies, biographical sketches, historical backgrounds — all these disciplines help us to better understand the Bible. But sometimes their focus is simply too narrow. From time to time, we need to step back and ask basic questions of the Bible. Not, "Are the locusts B-52 bombers?" but, "Why am I reading you?" Not, "What was the numerical significance of the 153 fish caught during the second miraculous catch of fish?" but, "Where are you taking me?"

The good news is that the Bible *is* taking us somewhere — from Genesis to Revelation, from Psalm 1 to 150, from the opening chapters of the Gospels to their conclusions. We are being invited to join a cast of travelers on the same journey. It is a journey from the Torah obedience of Psalm 1 (and Job 1) to the praise of Psalm 150, from thinking we know about God to at last seeing Him face-to-face. Every page turned is a step along this path. Every chapter is a mile marker along the way. The bad news is that this journey inevitably passes through the wilderness.

Every character we meet in the Bible is somewhere along this path. One travel narrative proceeds to another; each story is about leaving one place and going to the next, whether it is Abram leaving Ur or Joseph leaving Egypt or Jesus "resolutely setting His face for Jerusalem." Outside the gates of Eden, Adam and Eve leave to wander the fallen wilderness. Israel marches triumphantly out of Egypt on this same wilderness path that led through the desert of Shur, Sin, and Paran to the Promised Land. Later, they would limp away from the smoldering ruins of Jerusalem, forced to enter the lamenting path once more. As Jesus stumbles back along the road to Jerusalem, He who had learned the language of lament so well in the wilderness of His own life follows the path to Golgotha. There, He invites us to come out of the Egypt of our experience and worship Him in the wilderness.

The path to God is through the wilderness. There, and only there, will we learn what God is truly worth. There we discover His provision: manna, quail, living water. But more significantly, along this path we experience His Presence and discover it is more precious than His provision.

Israel saw the cloud of His Presence. Jesus heard His Voice. That same Presence urges us along the path of the journey through the wilderness. It is ever-present, whether we feel it or not. It always lingers before us, whether we perceive it or not.

At a time when worship seems a fluent language in the church, many have sensed a deeper reality waits in the wilderness. Only along this path through the wilderness will we experience the worth of God and thereby be enabled to "worth-ship" Him, for this is what the word truly means. To worship God is to celebrate His worth. And how can we know what He is worth unless we have met Him in the wilderness?

"Let my people go, so that they might worship me in the wilderness" (Exodus 7:16, JPS).

Moses, who spoke those pregnant words to the most powerful man in the known world, wrote for us only a single psalm. It is, not surprisingly, a lament. If you listen closely, you will hear the emotional echoes of the wilderness wanderings. It expresses a form of worship that is learned nowhere else.

Psalm 90

A prayer of Moses the man of God.

Lord, you have been our dwelling place
    throughout all generations.
Before the mountains were born
        or you brought forth the earth and the world,
        from everlasting to everlasting you are God.

You turn men back to dust,
> saying, "Return to dust, O sons of men."
For a thousand years in your sight
> are like a day that has just gone by,
> or like a watch in the night.
You sweep men away in the sleep of death;
> they are like the new grass of the morning—
though in the morning it springs up new,
> by evening it is dry and withered.
We are consumed by your anger
> and terrified by your indignation.
You have set our iniquities before you,
> our secret sins in the light of your presence.
All our days pass away under your wrath;
> we finish our years with a moan.
The length of our days is seventy years—
> or eighty, if we have the strength;
yet their span is but trouble and sorrow,
> for they quickly pass, and we fly away.
Who knows the power of your anger?
> For your wrath is as great as the fear that is due you.
Teach us to number our days aright,
> that we may gain a heart of wisdom.
Relent, O Lord! How long will it be?
> Have compassion on your servants.
Satisfy us in the morning with your unfailing love [hesed],
> that we may sing for joy and be glad all our days.
Make us glad for as many days as you have afflicted us,
> for as many years as we have seen trouble.
May your deeds be shown to your servants,
> your splendor to their children.
May the favor of the Lord our God rest upon us;
> establish the work of our hands for us—
yes, establish the work of our hands.

For Discussion

1. If the church today took wilderness worship more seriously, what would the impact look like?

2. We have more than enough examples of being called as individuals into the wilderness, but what about when a group or a congregation is called there?

For Meditation

1. What has God accomplished in your life through the wilderness?

2. Can you imagine making the leap from a relationship with God based on His provision to one rooted only in His presence?

9 | Morning and Mourning

Let me hear Your lovingkindness [hesed] in the morning.
PSALM 143:8, NASB

David, who spent more than his share of long, agonizing nights, knew that morning is the time when things inevitably change for the better (Psalm 5:3; 143:8). Even in the midst of his darkest, most mournful lament, Jeremiah recognized that morning was a special time to wait for the trustworthy appearance of the *hesed* of God (Lamentations 3:22-23). The appearance of his loving-kindness and compassionate faithfulness meant the end of mourning, for the time being. What makes morning unique is that it is the time when *hesed* appears.

They are both old, sturdy, Anglo-Saxon words: "morning" and "mourning." Despite the fact that they sound virtually the same, they descend from two completely different roots, as their spelling indicates. Yet they are inextricably linked in the Bible.

Though no translator in his right mind would render the verse this way, Psalm 30:5 could be translated, "Mourning may last for the night, but joy comes in the morning."

Perhaps what links the two words together is the fact that they both represent moments when we "wake up." Clearly morning is the time when we open our eyes to the hope of a new day; but in another, deeper sense, a time of mourning can also be an occasion when we "come to our senses" and with new, tear-cleansed eyes see the world as we have never seen it before.

When suffering wakes us up, lament leads us to a new understanding of who God is and what He means, or can mean, to us. The good news is that

He is fully present, both in the joy that comes in the morning as well as in the sorrow of mourning.

"Now is your time of grief," Jesus told His disciples just before He was arrested, "but I will see you again and you will rejoice, and no one will take away your joy" (John 16:22). That first Easter morning, as the disciples awoke from their sorrowful sleep, could they have ever dreamed of the greater joy to which they were about to awake — a joy that could only come to them in the morning, after their long night of unspeakable mourning?

For Discussion
1. How does suffering "wake us up"?
2. Discuss together the difference between happiness and the joy Jesus promised would never be taken away from us.

For Meditation
1. What was the state of your emotional life at the end of yesterday as opposed to this morning? Does the difference tell you anything?
2. What does this teaching do with your level of expectation in regard to the morning? In regard to mourning?

10 | A Most Dangerous Sanctuary

Curse God and die!
Job 2:9

I t was a clear July evening in Cape Town. The year was 1993. At Saint James Church, the announcements having just been read, the children were customarily dismissed to their classes. The congregation was opening the service, as usual, with a selection of special music.

My friend Larry Warren was struggling to make it to church that evening, but his wife, Mary, said she "didn't feel too well." And so she decided to stay home. Larry, determined to go, finally arrived ten minutes late. Finding his usual pew occupied, he took a seat in the back.

Just then, two men kicked in the side door of the church armed with AK–47s. They proceeded to spray the crowd with automatic weapons fire. When their magazines were empty they stepped aside to reload, giving the signal for two more men to toss hand grenades into the middle of the packed church. One grenade exploded next to the pew where my friend "should" have been sitting. Twelve people were killed. Fifty-three were wounded.

In the intervening years Larry has faced such danger again and again. Most recently he was kidnapped while his wife and seven-year-old son were held for ransom. No one was harmed.

Whenever we can convince Larry to tell his story, in his own taciturn way he always concludes, "The safest place to be is right where the Lord wants you." Sometimes the safest place is the most dangerous place.

As he barely clings to life, Job cries out to God his sorrow, his disappointment, his outrage, and his fear. Perhaps more than anyone in the Bible, he was learning just how dangerous a place the world can be: dangerous for your children, dangerous because of terrorists, dangerous because of the disease that is always waiting around the next corner or even perhaps lurking in one of the cells in your own body. The hand grenades and machine gun fire were going off all around Job but God had not been late for a single bullet. It is out of the explosive darkness of the shadows of this dangerous world that Job speaks his lament.

In all probability Job did not know the story of the nameless son of Shelomith who, in Leviticus 24:10-23, blasphemed the Name of God and was put to death, but the principle behind the story was apparently clear to everyone. Job's friends believe it (15:13). Certainly Job's wife understands this idea and out of her love for her tormented husband begs him to speak the blasphemous words that will end his life . . . that will end his pain (2:9). But God has given Job a freedom to say what he feels he needs to say . . . and Job somehow knows he has been given this freedom.

> "He may well slay me; I may have no hope,
>> Yet I will argue my case before Him.
>> *In this too is my salvation.*" (13:15-16, JPS, my italics)

Job knew that an even more dangerous place was looming before him, beyond the shadows of the fallen world. He was being pulled toward it by two gravitational forces: his love for God and his argument with God. He was being irresistibly drawn into the Presence. Step by step, the costly words of his lament were leading him there. Saying more than he could possibly know or understand, still Job realizes that somewhere beyond the smoke and shadows of this difficult dialogue, his salvation is waiting.

By definition, the place where Job is heading is a sanctuary, perhaps *the* Sanctuary. The word comes from the Latin *sanctus*, or "holy." A sanctuary is a place where we find holiness. In the past, wiser and more spiritual men often spoke of this place existing on the other side of a dark cloud, a "cloud of unknowing."

So it might be said that in the end it is all simply a matter of the nature of holiness, of how we perceive the holiness of God. If Job's wife and his friends are right, then we should mind every word lest we somehow violate this holiness. Any indiscretion could lead to death.

But if Job is right, if David and Jeremiah and Jesus are right, then we have been granted an indescribable freedom of access to the Sanctuary, to the immediate Presence. And in that place we have the promise of being heard — not just tolerated, but intensely and compassionately listened to. If His holiness is defined by *hesed*, by loving-kindness, then this must define the atmosphere of our prayers of lament. This is not to say that it is still not a dangerous place, for God remains an awesome God. But the nature of His holiness provides security in the Sanctuary. We come with confidence, trusting that we are safe here, before the throne of God. He has bid us to enter in, giving us the words if we cannot find them. It is not safe. He is not safe, but He is good.

For Discussion

1. Contrast the two ideas about the holiness of God from your own experience.
2. What would a life look like lived out in this sort of awareness of the intimacy we are promised with God?

For Meditation

1. If you are in a cloud of confusion right now, imagine that God is waiting for you on the other side of that confusion.
2. In one sense, something indeed does die in Job's life. What is it?

Part Two

A Place for the Poor and the Prisoner

11 | Good News to the Poor

I have come to preach good news to the poor.
LUKE 4:18

Those were the very first words Jesus spoke at the start of His ministry, and so they are the perfect words, simply because He spoke them. But they were not easily spoken. They were costly words. In the end, they would cost Him everything. His followers would fret, "If only He would have had the good sense to identify with the rich and the powerful instead of the poor. If only He had acted in accordance with their values. If only He had danced to their tune . . ." But Jesus did not, would not, dance (Luke 7:32).

There are no words to describe the extent to which He radically identified with the poor. In one of two disturbing and surprising moments that are yet to come, Jesus said, in effect: When you fed the poor, you were feeding Me. When you neglected them, you were neglecting Me. This is one-on-one identification. "If they reject you, they are rejecting Me." The absolute Highness standing with the lowest.

In a religious world that had concluded that the poor were poor because they were sinners and cursed by God as a result, Jesus came and paradoxically pronounced on them God's blessing. "Blessed are you who are poor," He said, because this world is not the only world that exists, and an upside-down kingdom is coming where rich and poor will change places, where those who weep will laugh and the laughing ones will burst into tears. That world is here and at the same time, it is coming.

This is not to say that Jesus didn't have a few wealthy friends, Joseph of Arimathea being the most noteworthy. But by and large He gravitated toward the poor, and they were drawn almost gravitationally to Him. They followed Him in droves, not necessarily because they grasped fully what His life meant, or what the gospel was, but because they recognized in Him a compassionate heart that would feed them if He could, even when He was forced to borrow bread and fish from a hungry little boy to do so.

Even those who, because of their lack of education, were unaware of Isaiah's prophecy that He would be a Man of Sorrows acquainted with our deepest grief recognized in Him someone whose tears were somehow their tears as well. He was not only weeping for them, He was weeping with them, becoming acquainted to the darkest depths with their poverty and pain.

Jesus had made it clear that He was going to raise his friend Lazarus, and yet when He saw Lazarus's sister Mary in tears, initially He could do nothing but weep with her. He did not explain away the pain, did not say He had come with the answer, that He would fix everything; no, He bowed His head and allowed the tears to flow. It was not about providing answers or fixing a problem, it was about entering fully and redemptively into her suffering. Jesus did not weep because it was the right or the sympathetic thing to do. He did it because the shape of His heart would not allow him to do otherwise. Jesus knew that God uses suffering to save the world. He had not come to fix death and sorrow but to ultimately bring about their demise. He had not come to give answers; He had come to give Himself. His presence, His tears were the solution, the answer, the Truth for that painful moment, perhaps more than the resuscitating of Lazarus; for, after all, that would only be a temporary reprieve. And in the midst of that moment, Mary didn't get what she wanted, not just yet, but she got exactly what she needed.

Before the Man of Sorrows wept, Job became acquainted with all-out grief. Job's experience was just the same. He had lost everything a person can lose — his possessions (that was the easy part), his children, his health. He was exposed to every fear, from the terrorism of the Sabeans to the hopeless anguish of cancer, or perhaps some other wasting disease like Ebola. He tasted the despair of losing his children. Most painful of all, he thought he had lost his God, or perhaps even worse, that his God had abandoned him.

So how does this apply? What does Jesus' redemptive weeping have to do with us? The answer is, it has everything to do with us. Our call is not to fix those who weep, but to weep with them. We don't need funds or expertise.

We are not expected to provide every individual answer, each solution. Those who seek in obedience to follow Jesus don't pretend to have all the answers. We don't pretend to be able to fix every problem and dry every tear — but we can weep. And our tears uniquely qualify us for mission.

After all, fixing people is God's work. The Father is more deeply committed to it — to fixing all of us, rich and poor — than we could imagine. But fixing isn't the right word for it; the Bible's word is salvation, re-creation. We don't need to be fixed; we need to be re-created. The only way we, all of us, will ever experience that re-creation is to open the door of our lives to the poor, to enter redemptively into their suffering, and to discover through it our suffering as well. They are weeping our tears; Jesus in them is weeping our tears.

So celebrate the tears, the frustration, the confusion. Celebrate every day that you are tempted to give up but don't. Celebrate changed lives, re-created lives, saved souls, men and women who have discovered that they are not alone after all, children who have discovered that there is a place in a family just for them after all. Be glad with us that good news has come to the poor, as a special blessing to all of us who labor and are heavy-laden. He is worthy of such gladness. In the meantime, continue to weep with those who weep; enter redemptively into the suffering that comes to your door.

For Discussion

1. As a group, discuss the possibility of opening the door of your life to one person who lives at the poverty level.
2. List and discuss some of the lessons the poor have to teach us.

For Meditation

1. In Jesus' eyes, who is not poor?
2. Meditate on what you can remember of the ministry of Jesus, understanding it afresh in the light of His opening purpose statement.

12 | Confusion and Clarity, Poverty and Presence

For I was hungry, and you fed me. I was thirsty, and you gave me a drink.
I was a stranger, and you invited me into your home. I was naked,
and you gave me clothing. I was sick, and you cared for me.
I was in prison, and you visited me.
MATTHEW 25:35-36, NLT

In the past few years, for hundreds of thousands of people all over the globe, it has seemed like the end of the world. Their homes have been swept away by angry walls of water. Little ones have been wrenched from the arms of panicked parents. People who already had little were left with absolutely nothing. The bitter confusion caused by a tsunami on the other side of the world and the venomous blame-shifting that resulted from hurricane Katrina on this side, left some of us wondering where God stood in the whole mystifying matter.

To the poor who have been left childless and homeless, it must seem as if God broke His promise never to destroy the world again by water (Genesis 9:15). Their world, at least, *was* destroyed. These two major disasters serve to simply lift the veil on the suffering that goes on in the world every single day. More children die of hunger (and have been dying for decades) every day than were lost in the last hurricane. More Christians have been swept away by persecution in the last few years than died in the tsunami. Now it seems our fresh voices of lament are simply joining the already hoarse cries of the rest of the world, asking God for a way out of the confusion.

At first glance, the Bible seems to say there is no single way out. There is no unified answer that will sweep the suffering of the world under the carpet. It is a fallen and death-invaded world—it has been so since the expulsion from the garden, and it will remain so until Christ returns. Decay and chaos, disease and death are the rules in nature.

Look hard at the teaching of Jesus and you'll find neither an outline nor an answer. He ultimately offers no quick fixes, no certain aid. But what Jesus unquestionably offers in the Gospels is *Himself*. There is an Answer. He tells us that if there is a way, it is He (John 14:6). It is left to us to understand just what that means and what it implies as we look at our devastated world.

When we see the pattern of His perfect life, we begin to understand that while Jesus consistently provided for the practical needs He saw (healing or perhaps food), more important, He always provided Himself. He was fully present to the suffering of His friends (John 11:33-35). In effect, He became one of them. He entered redemptively into the confusion and pain He seemed to attract like a magnet (Luke 7:11-17,36-50). He fully identified with the sinful woman, with the poor beggar, even with the confused Pharisee. Most of all, Jesus entered fully and effectively into the pain and confusion created by our sin. When He suffered and died on the cross, He paid the full price for becoming one of us. Long before anyone in Indonesia or the gulf coast cried out, "Why have You forsaken me?" Jesus lamented these words for them and for us.

If His life can be seen as a sort of compass—that is to say, if there is a direction indicated in the truth that Jesus is the "Way"—then that direction is to move *into* the suffering of the world and into our own suffering. If anything can push back the confusion, it will be His Presence mediated through our own presence among the shattered lives we increasingly find all around us.

Jesus spoke about another time of confusion that is coming. It will occur at the bona fide end of the world, upon His Second Coming. As Jesus prepares to enter into the hurricane of pain and the tsunami of suffering that will soon wash over Him in the garden and on the cross, He paints a confusing picture for His disciples.

"Then these righteous ones will reply, 'Lord, when did we ever see you hungry and feed you? Or thirsty and give you something to drink? Or a stranger and show you hospitality? Or naked and give you clothing? When did we ever see you sick or in prison, and visit you?' And the King will say, 'I tell you the truth, when you did it to one of the least of these my brothers and sisters, you were doing it to me!'

"Then the King will turn to those on the left and say, 'Away with you, you cursed ones, into the eternal fire prepared for the devil and his demons. For I was hungry, and you didn't feed me. I was thirsty, and you didn't give me a drink. I was a stranger, and you didn't invite me into your home. I was naked, and you didn't give me clothing. I was sick and in prison, and you didn't visit me.'

"Then they will reply, 'Lord, when did we ever see you hungry or thirsty or a stranger or naked or sick or in prison, and not help you?' And he will answer, 'I tell you the truth, when you refused to help the least of these my brothers and sisters, you were refusing to help me.'" (Matthew 25:37-45, NLT)

As the "sheep and goats" stand before the King for their final sorting, the major dividing line seems to be whether or not they cared for the poor. This should seem self-evident to almost any religious person, but what is most strange about Jesus' telling of the story is that both groups are in a state of confusion.

The first group had, in fact, cared for the poor and the prisoner and the sick. But they seem confused when Jesus announced that it was really He to whom they had ministered. He does not say "it was *like* you were ministering to Me." No, Jesus radically identifies Himself with the sorrowing. This idea is precisely where the ministry of Mother Teresa derived its amazing power.

The final confusion exists among the group who did not care for the poor, the goats. When they refused these least ones, they were refusing Jesus Himself. I am forced to believe that this is the same surprised and confused group Jesus spoke about in Matthew 7:22. They had done all sorts of "works" — prophesied, exorcised, and so on. And yet Jesus says, "I never knew you."

That final end-of-the-world state of confusion we read about in Matthew sheds an enormous amount of light upon our present state of confusion. The call of Jesus becomes crystal clear precisely at the meeting of these two states of bewilderment. We are to provide food, drink, clothing, hospitality, and visitations to those in prison, realizing that we will never reach the bottom of the bottomless needs of the world. But in so doing, we can enter redemptively into the suffering of the fallen, confused, and hurting world, there to find . . . Jesus Himself.

For Discussion
1. As a group, discuss what you can do for those who suffer from devastating disasters without leaving your own town.
2. How can we make certain that we will not be among the second confused group at the Coming of Jesus?

For Meditation
1. What is the true "way out" of any disaster?
2. Can you really become a part of the suffering voice of the world? If so, how?

13 | A Different Cross

There is a different cross for the Church in the West.

Brother Yun

I f you're like me, every time you hear the testimonies that come from the persecuted Church you become aware of a deep sense of guilt and shame. Unfortunately, many overseas mission groups twist this dagger in order to make us respond to their legitimate appeals for financial support. The needs *are* legitimate, but the means to meet the needs often seem manipulative.

Recently, I read David Hunt's remarkable little book *The Heavenly Man*. It tells the story of a young man, Yun, who comes to faith in China, receives the call to serve Christ, and suffers unimaginably for his faithfulness. David's account presents the powerful story in forthright simplicity, without producing the slightest hint of guilt. Brother Yun's experience of torture and solitary confinement over the years has led those in the underground Church to regard him as perhaps the most persecuted believer in China, a mark of reverence that he would undoubtedly despise. David tells his complete story, including his miraculous release from prison as well as those moments when he had sunk so low that he complained to God in prayer. His genuine struggles in following the impossible and scandalous call of Jesus flow seamlessly into scenes of his childlike faith, which literally opened prison doors and healed the deaf and the blind. Brother Yun's life is as near a perfect response as we will likely see to the question, "What should a follower of Jesus do in the face of persecution?"

I found Brother Yun's answer, powerfully incarnate in his own suffering life, both disturbingly clear and wonderfully comforting. I learned long ago that when Christ breaks through, all our old concepts are shattered and redefined. Brother Yun said, "The people who are in prison are not the ones who are suffering, but the ones in the West who are free." He said that we, in our freedom, are the ones who are truly suffering in a spiritual sense. "The real people who suffer are the ones who never experience God's presence. . . . there is a different cross for the Church in the West."

Before, when I would hear such stories, I would shrug my shoulders, hang my head, and limp in the other direction, away from the gospel. But now, in the light of Yun's life, I am left to struggle with a new set of questions in terms shattered and redefined. His life is an answer to the question, "What does a disciple do in the face of persecution?" What I'm beginning to realize is that the question does not, cannot, apply to those of us in the West who know no real persecution. The question we should seek to answer with our lives is, "What does a disciple do in the face of freedom?" The answer to the first question is ringing loudly in China and elsewhere from the persecuted Church. But the time has come, not from guilt but from our place of freedom, to answer the second question for ourselves. We know what they have done with their poverty. What will we do with our wealth? We know how faithfully they have suffered. But what does faithfulness look like when lived out in the context of comfort? If Yun is right and the West truly has a different cross, what does the faithful carrying of that cross look like?

Brother Yun, whose unspeakable experiences in torture chambers and prisons should qualify him to provide the most reliable of all definitions of the word suffering, radically redefines the word for those of us in the West. We must strain with all that is within us to hear and understand as Christ speaks through him to us: Real suffering comes from not knowing God's presence.

In the face of our freedom, wealth, and comfort, Satan would have us guiltily toss a few coins in the plate, feeling all the more guilt that we do not demonstrate our faith in the face of persecution as those in China and elsewhere. What I believe Brother Yun would encourage us, with tears, to do is take up the cross that's been given to the West, the cross of a perceived absence of God's presence, and to speak boldly to our sisters and brothers (and to ourselves!) who have so long felt cut off because of our comfort, who have been weakened by the immensity of our wealth, who have taken for granted our freedom.

I pray that someday soon we might astonish our persecuted brothers and sisters with the magnitude of our response to their suffering — that the impact of our prayers, spoken in security, would be felt throughout the suffering Church; that the experience of profound relief, from the excess of our financial riches, given in joy, would provide them a moment's comfort, a cup of cold water.

For Discussion

1. As a group, discuss how you can become involved in comforting the persecuted Church around the world (see, for example, www.worldserve.org).

2. What are some of the legitimate crosses we bear? Name some "illegitimate" ones.

For Meditation

1. In one sentence, describe what you have learned from pastor Yun about your own suffering.

2. Imagine facing genuine persecution for your own faith in Jesus. Where would you turn for strength to endure?

14 | Fellow Prisoners

*Remember those in prison as if you were their fellow prisoners, and those
who are mistreated as if you yourselves were suffering.*

HEBREWS 13:3

I am writing to you from just outside the city of Jinan, in northern China.
Along with friends from WorldServe, I have been visiting some of the leaders in the underground Church. WorldServe is a ministry that serves believers in closed and restricted countries by simply coming alongside them and
listening to their needs. But during the past week here in China and Vietnam,
I've begun to discover that listening is neither simple nor easy.

It is not easy to listen to the stories of suffering you frequently hear in
this place — stories of torture, and prison, and persecution. In one of our first
meetings, we spoke to some brothers who were concerned about a couple of
women from their community who had been imprisoned along with their
young children. One brother (we call him snowman) had been chained to a
wall in the prison yard in the dead of winter. The guards watched through the
window, warm inside, waiting for him to succumb to the cold. Finally, as dark
fell, they decided it was easier to leave him there for the night to make sure he
was "finished."

The next morning, as they approached the still suspended body, they
noticed steam rising from it. Miraculously, he had survived the night's expo-
sure to sub-zero cold.

That same winter two young women, who had been thrown out of their
home for embracing Jesus, were wandering from house to house in their village
asking to be taken in. Like the Holy Family, they discovered that no one would

make room. To shelter the new converts would bring guilt by association.

Finally, they quietly whispered, "We lay down in the snow. We had lost all hope and decided to 'fall asleep' in the drifting snow."

When they woke up the next morning, warm and unharmed by the winter chill, they noticed small footprints all around them in the snow. It became apparent to them both that small animals had come in the night and lain next to the two girls, keeping them warm.

Again and again we heard these kinds of stories, stories of suffering and the remarkable intervention of God, saving believers not from the suffering, but through it. One man told us that though he had been tortured several times, he felt no pain during the beatings. Another older brother we called "tire man," had his hands ripped to shreds by the nylon strands in the tires he was forced to pull apart in prison. With another one of those gentle smiles I became used to experiencing, he showed me his hands. They had healed almost scar-free.

Not all the stories end with miraculous interventions or healings. Many have died in prison. Many more wander the streets, having been forced out of their homes only because their association with the underground Church was exposed by neighbors and, incredibly, sometimes by members of their own families.

> By faith these people overthrew kingdoms, ruled with justice, and received what God had promised them. They shut the mouths of lions, quenched the flames of fire, and escaped death by the edge of the sword. Their weakness was turned to strength. They became strong in battle and put whole armies to flight. Women received their loved ones back again from death.
>
> But others trusted God and were tortured, preferring to die rather than turn from God and be free. They placed their hope in the resurrection to a better life. Some were mocked, and their backs were cut open with whips. Others were chained in dungeons. Some died by stoning, and some were sawed in half; others were killed with the sword. Some went about in skins of sheep and goats, hungry and oppressed and mistreated. They were too good for this world. They wandered over deserts and mountains, hiding in caves and holes in the ground. (Hebrews 11:33-38, NLT)

Hebrews 11:33-38 contains a list of both those who win and those who lose. By faith some of them conquered kingdoms, stopped the mouths of lions, and quenched the fury of the flames. But others were mocked and flogged, stoned, and even sawn in two. Like the believers in China, all were called to suffer for their faith. Though some might not have been miraculously "delivered," all of them were winners by the simple fact that they overcame by grace through their faith in Jesus.

If you think I'm going to spin the story to manipulate you into feeling guilty or inferior in your faith because you have not experienced prison, you're wrong. What I'm campaigning for is your *presence*. The hunger I'd like to awaken in your heart is simply to "be there" in prayer alongside the brothers and sisters, some of whose stories I've been telling. It does not necessitate the seven thousand mile plane ride I made to get here.

The same unknown author of Hebrews who gave us the list of the winners and losers (who in the end were all winners), ended his "brief letter" with a benediction. Call it the key, or the starting place, call it anything you want, but within that benediction he opens the door to a whole new world of prayer — the prayer of *presence*. "Remember (in prayer) those in prison as if you were their fellow prisoners," he said. Prayer as an extension of your presence, of your being there, not prayer for miraculous deliverance or healing (though these are still appropriate requests to make), but prayer that, in faith, projects your presence into those prison cells in China, Vietnam, Sudan, El Salvador, Pakistan, Iraq, and Iran . . . the list goes on. More believers are dying for Christ in this present day than at any time in the history of the Church. One believer in China spoke in tears, "I thought you had forgotten us."

Remember those who are in prison, and in your remembering, by faith, be there for them, be *present*. In your prayer, open the door of your life to their suffering, not that their laments might end, but so they will know they do not lament alone.

For Discussion

1. Discuss the implications that more Christians are behind bars for their faith in Jesus today than at any time in the history of the Church.

2. What are some of the lessons you might learn in prison that you cannot learn anywhere else?

For Meditation

1. Through prayer, ask that your heart might connect to just one person who is in prison for his or her faith.

2. Meditate on those things that imprison you today.

15 | Tears of the World

Weep with those who weep.
ROMANS 12:15, NASB

In a makeshift marketplace in the middle of Jakarta, my friend Scott Roley wanders amidst a confusing crowd of the hopeless, who stagger in shock, and the hopeful, who have come highly motivated to offer what help they can.

Two weeks earlier a 9.2 magnitude earthquake off the west coast of Sumatra pushed up a wall of water that obliterated villages along the shores of ten different countries, the wave finally dying out on the far-off eastern coast of Africa. So far the number of dead has been reckoned at 270,000, but that number is deceiving, since over 100,000 are still missing and will tragically remain so.

Jakarta has become one of the cities of refuge for those in the hardest hit area of the nearby province of Banda Ache. The town is a rallying point as well for scores of relief agencies. Scott, who helps direct the mission resources of our church, was there meeting with missionaries, gathering as much information as he could to report back to the fellowship on how we might best serve the victims of the nameless disaster. He had come to "the ends of the earth" to represent those who could not come but who nonetheless cared and wanted to help.

Finally, overcome by the mind-boggling scope of the pain and need, by the seeming hopelessness of so many hundreds of thousands, and by his own physical and emotional exhaustion, he sat down on one of the crowded curbs.

As his mind began to resurface from the confusion, Scott became aware of a man sitting next to him. Like countless others, he had lost everything a person could lose — his wife, all his children, and his home. They had all been swept away. Nothing was left. None of them could be found.

Scott placed a hand on the stranger's shoulder and, without a word, together the two of them began to weep. After a time the man turned his face toward Scott and whispered, "You must be a Christian." With that, he straightened up, turned, and disappeared into the sea of people.

There was no dramatic conversion experience for this Muslim man, not yet anyway. His own people had violently driven the Christians from Banda Ache only a few years before. Already some of their leaders were beginning to preach that the tsunami was a punishment from God for not completely wiping out the Christians.

Moved by the staggering need and thoughtless of their own personal safety, the Christians were coming back into the area from which they had been driven to serve their persecutors. The unexpected brilliance of the light of their faith as seen in their sincere and unqualified love had begun to push back the darkness the tsunami had left in its wake. Along with hammers and saws, shovels and Bibles, one of their most effective tools for this impossible mission, as Scott discovered, was *tears*.

"Weep with those who weep" (Romans 12:15, NASB). Paul wrote those words to the believers in Rome around AD 56. The purpose of his letter to the Romans is almost universally misunderstood. It is usually thought of as a great work of theology, which it certainly is. But that is not why Paul wrote the letter. The simple fact is, Paul was a missionary, and he was on his way to Spain, which the Romans referred to as Iberia, literally "the ends of the earth." The reason Paul wrote was to prepare the church at Rome for his upcoming visit on the way to Spain and to hopefully receive their support for his mission. New Testament scholar William Lane called Romans a "missionary manifesto." Paul outlines his understanding of the gospel not only to teach the church but also to demonstrate the nature of his missionary message.

Appropriately enough, it is in one of his great passages on love that Paul talks about tears. The section opens with the words, "love must be sincere" (Romans 12:9) and follows with a long list of just what sincere love looks like when it is lived out according to the gospel. Halfway through that list, Paul writes that one of the signs of the sincerity of love is to "weep with those who weep." In the midst of the most profound missional statement of the gospel of Jesus . . . tears.

Tears are nothing new, certainly. Before there were drops of rain there were human tears. They are the defining reality of living in a death-infested, fallen world. The Bible says that even the world around us is groaning with the weight of the sorrow. But in light of Paul's statement, we see that tears can have a divine purpose. They can become meaningful as they become a vehicle for communicating the sincere love of the gospel of Christ. In Him is the omniscient compassion of the God who knows of each and every human sorrow — from the child on some nameless, remote island who is this very minute calling out for her mother who was washed out to sea, to the homeless man, living only a couple of miles from where I am at this minute, who weeps for the children he let slip through his fingers due to some addiction. As God, Jesus *knows* the depth of each of these bottomless pools of grief. As man, he is able to bring up, call forth, perhaps not even be able to hold back — tears. His contemporaries heard Him break into weeping more than once. Through the Incarnation, the tear that was poised in the eye of the world found expression as it coursed down the dark cheek of Jesus' face.

Though there will always be that side of me that would rather not weep — would rather not "go there" — there is another, newer part that longs to weep these sorts of redemptive tears of and for the world. In the midst of all the confusion and pain, what seems abundantly clear to me is that only through Jesus of Nazareth, only through looking to Him and walking with Him, will we ever be able to connect redemptively with the world's sorrow. Because on the cross He showed us how sorrow can save the world.

And so my best friend found himself in a crowded marketplace at "the ends of the earth." He had been sent by a large, wealthy congregation as an expression of their love. Though Scott's recommendation could bring to bear tens of thousands of badly needed dollars, in that moment tears were his greatest resource, the most powerful demonstration of the sincerity of the body of Christ's love.

For Discussion

1. If it were indeed possible for your group to weep the tears of the world, how would your lives change? What would be the impact on your value system?

2. The word compassion literally means to "suffer with." How and to what extent is it possible to actualize the meaning of this word as a Christian community?

For Meditation

1. What is the message that is spoken by means of wordless tears?

2. Imagine that you are in a place like Jakarta. How would the fact that you belong to Jesus Christ be made evident even if you never opened your mouth?

16 | A Bottle of Tears

You put my tears in Your bottle.
PSALM 56:8, NASB

Just this morning my youngest daughter, Maggie, came to me cradling a twisted strip of pink plastic in her hands. She had found it in the bottom of a large box in the attic marked "Maggie."

"What is it?" She asked.

As I looked at it more closely I read in small stamped letters, "CARD, BABY GIRL." A flood of memories rushed over me when I realized it was the bracelet the nurse in the delivery room had placed around her wrist the moment she was born.

I explained what it was, remembering for her, in as much detail as I could muster up, what it was like for me to see her small face for the first time, to be the first person to hold her. But I began to notice that my teary remembrances didn't seem to resonate with her in the least. As she kept turning the bracelet over and over in her small hands she looked up and whispered, "Mom saved this?" It wasn't my paternal moment from thirteen years ago that captured her imagination. It was the fact that her mother had cared enough to save even this tiny scrap of her past, to value it as a treasured keepsake.

Psalm 56:8 speaks of a God who treasures away such keepsakes. The verse contains a key word which translators seem fairly evenly divided on. It is the Hebrew word *node*. This is one of those instances in which, once you understand the background, you can make a choice for yourself as well as the scholars.

Node is from an uncertain root word that has something to do with skin.

So here are your choices:

First it can be translated "scroll," since scrolls were made from animal skins. The problem is, a couple of other words are used to designate "scroll" in the Old Testament (Ezekiel 3:1 and Isaiah 34:4), not *node*. This choice is, however, supported by the second phrase of the verse, which makes it read as a parallel: "List my tears on Your *scroll*, are they not in Your *book*?" Parallelism — often used for emphasis — is the most common literary device in Hebrew poetry. So perhaps it is a poetic echo and nothing more.

The second choice is to see the word as referring to a wine*skin* or flask. *Node* occurs twice in the Old Testament with this meaning, in 1 Samuel 16:20 and Judges 4:19 (see Jesus' teaching in Matthew 9:17 and Mark 2:22). Also in support of this translation are thousands of tiny, long-necked bottles archaeologists have unearthed all over Israel called "lachrymatories," or "tear bottles." Supporters of the second translation choice point to these as the best cultural support of their position. Those inside the first "scroll" camp say these bottles were merely for expensive perfume. This is just a tiny window into the confusing world of the Bible translator.

Either way, the text is saying that our tears are of great value to God. He takes the time to record each one on a scroll or in a book, or else He treasures them enough to collect them in a bottle as precious as perfume.

I confess I tend to gravitate toward the second choice. I like the notion that God has a bottle and a book. An infinitely compassionate meteorologist, He collects and records our tears, measuring and recording "tearfall."

When you step back and look at the psalm, you might be surprised to discover that it is one of the "warrior psalms" of David, sung to the long lost tune of "A Dove on Distant Oaks." In this psalm, David is lamenting to God about the battle he is having with his numerous enemies, both within his kingdom and without. They plot and conspire and twist his words. David has had all he can stand and cries out for mercy (verse 1). It is Israel's fearless warrior king who pleads with God, but he is a weeping warrior. In the midst of his turmoil he finds comfort in the image of the God who bends to compassionately collect his tears in a flask and make note of them in His special scroll.

But this, I believe, is not the main source of comfort and encouragement David finds in singing this song of the God of the bottle and the book. The key is a twice-repeated phrase. In verses four and eleven David writes:

I am not afraid; what can mortals do to me? (JPS).

It is a phrase that echoes in the New Testament in the benediction of Hebrews 13:6. If you listen carefully you can detect that the tone is more a matter of simple, childlike trust than complicated, grown-up theology. It is a confidence rooted in the memory of the little boy who once stood before an unconquerable giant with only five smooth stones in his pocket. On that long-ago battlefield, God taught David that mere mortals indeed could not harm him. Now, in the midst of yet another long line of battles, he turns over in his mind, again and again, the image of the leather lachrymatory and amazed, reaches out through lament to the God who cares deeply enough to make a keepsake of a collection of his tears.

For Discussion
1. As a group, discuss the merits of each alternate translation of the passage above.
2. Is the statement about the bottle and the book hyperbole or an understatement of an even more intense concern?

For Meditation
1. Try to imagine the level of intimacy expressed in God's concern for our tears. Is there a human relationship in your experience that even comes close?
2. Meditate on the power of a weeping warrior.

17 | How Long?

Lord, how long will this go on?
PSALM 6:3

The psalmists' questions sound like waves exhausting themselves over time against a great rock:

How long will You look on? (35:17)

How long, O God, will the adversary hurl insults? (74:10)

How long, O Lord, will You be angry? (79:5)

How long will Your wrath burn like fire? (89:46)

Sooner or later, practically every one of the psalmists asks this question. Perhaps each knows how desperately we needed him to ask it for all of us. In the list above, the first two quotes are from David, the third and fourth from Asaph and the fifth from Ethan the Ezrahite. Together with the question "Why?," "How long?" is the fundamental question of lament. "*Why* have You acted in a way so inconsistent with *hesed*?" and "*How long* until You show up, wake up, rouse Yourself, O God, and act according to Your own revelation of Yourself?"

More than forty years ago on a summer afternoon, in the back of the Vista Cruiser, my sister Caroline said, "Your greatest strength is your greatest weakness." We were both still young children. It was one of those moments when a person says infinitely more than they know. Her little motto has become a lens through which I've looked at the world ever since. It is true; the "strengths" of the beautiful woman or the virtuoso or the millionaire businessman can and usually do become their greatest weaknesses. More often than not, they are the reason for their downfall. Think of the most famous, wealthy, and beautiful people in this or any other time: the Dianas, the Michael Jacksons, all the kings from Henry VIII to Croesus. But for a few examples, they have all been destroyed by what were seen by the world as their greatest strengths. Their beauty made them ugly. Their wealth robbed their lives of value.

The same holds true in regard to each of us when it comes to time. We possess just as much of it as any billionaire. It could be our greatest strength simply because anything worthwhile we will ever accomplish must be done "in" time. But, true to the motto, time also becomes our enemy, because all that is unworthy happens within its walls as well. Moreover, the wasting of time is an expression of our greatest weakness as we sit before the TV or the computer screen, pouring out the expensive perfume of our lives on the ground.

When it comes to the daily-ness of time, God, who so often seems to be so inequitable in the giving out of gifts, has leveled the playing field by giving to each one of us precisely the same amount: 23 hours, 56 minutes, 4.1 seconds in a day. It's up to us to treasure or trash these moments. It is up to us to recognize them as gifts or despise them by pouring them out on the ground.

We are most tempted to despise time when we are in the midst of suffering, or when we are witnessing the suffering of those we love. The clock slows down or stops altogether. The pain, physical or emotional, becomes concentrated and interminable. At those moments, I experience a particular panic: the fear that it is never going to stop.

These are not the times when most of us wax eloquent, searching for just the right adjectives to describe the suffering. By and large, two words will do. How long?

How long before the pain stops?

How long do I have to witness this suffering?

How long until You show up, O Lord?

While we are waiting for the miracle, it is easy to miss the deeper, more trustworthy miracle that lies underneath these two words — the miracle of lament, which is the miracle of faith. It happens when the sufferer still finds within himself the faith to spend what is left of that precious time calling out to a God who, at that moment, couldn't seem to be more remote. The miracle of crying for help — not to some void, but to the One who is beyond the void.

To lament is to reach out across the unreachable to the Unreachable One. The frustrated, disappointed, suffering scream that is at the same moment a miraculous cry of faith. It is the miracle behind the miracle.

Of all the psalmists who ever called out these two desolate words, only Moses, who knew more about suffering and time than any of us, attempts a fragmented answer. Psalm 90, the only psalm of Moses we have, is appropriately enough a lament. In verse 13, Moses cries, "How long?" (In the next verse he calls out for *hesed*.)

Earlier, in verse 4, amidst a passage of dark praise for God, he had spoken a tiny shard of an answer to his own question. It is the great statement of scale that we so badly needed. I wonder if he was listening to himself as he said it: "A thousand years in your sight are like a day."

A thousand years later, it is Simon Peter who finds comfort in this unthinkable scale. In his last letter, as he wondered "how long" it would be before he heard the executioner's footsteps coming to crucify him, he addresses what is left of his little flock. They had been caught up in their own lament: "How long until the Day of the Lord?"

After quoting Moses, Peter adds his own simple understanding to the problem of the unanswerable question. In 2 Peter 3:9 he reassures, "The Lord is not slow in keeping his promise, as some understand slowness."

"As *some* understand slowness." That is you and me. We are the "some" of Simon's statement. Everyone who cries out "How long?" has mistaken the Lord's patience (a dimension of His *hesed*) for slowness. It is not really the answer, anymore than Moses' words. Even less when we are in the midst of suffering. Perhaps because God knows that when we are in the midst of suffering, answers are not what we need most.

How long before the pain goes away? . . . no answer.

How long before my loved one dies of cancer? . . . no answer.

Just because God refuses to answer this question, as Jesus refused to answer it (Mark 13:32), it does not mean that we should stop asking, "How long?" Even if we do give up, the psalms will keep on asking it for us. The question keeps us connected when nothing else will hold. It is a frame around the unanswerable silence. It creates a space that will be filled, sooner or later, by the One who is not slow after all, but infinitely patient.

For Discussion

1. Make a list together of your greatest strengths. Now discuss how they can become your greatest weaknesses.

2. What does it reveal about God that He was willing to enter time for us? What limitations did Jesus take on in doing so?

For Meditation

1. What happens to time when we suffer? When we experience joy?

2. Imagine heaven as a place outside of time. When we leave this world to go to heaven, we leave time behind as well.

18 | The Listening and Lamenting Flock

I am the good shepherd. I know my own and my own know me, just as the Father knows me and I know the Father; and I lay down my life for the sheep. And I have other sheep that are not of this fold. I must bring them also, and they will listen to my voice. So there will be one flock, one shepherd.

JOHN 10:14-16, ESV

istening:

The two of them are huddled together in a small tent, trying to escape an unexpected dust storm. Occasionally one of the miserable sheep standing outside would bleat.

"That is Yamin," the old shepherd says.

And then later, "Oh, that is Rakak."

On one of his frequent mission trips to the Middle East, my friend had met the shepherd with whom he was now taking refuge. They had first met on the road outside a small village in northern Israel. The middle-aged man was gathering the flock from one of the barren hillsides. As my friend watched in amazement the shepherd literally called each of the sheep by name. Now, in the middle of the windstorm, he was even more astonished to realize that the shepherd knew the sound of each of their voices.

Matthew speaks of the compassion (*hesed* in Old Testament Hebrew) of Jesus as he looked at the crowd of people who were flocking to Him (Matthew 9:35-36). This statement follows a reference to one of Jesus' run-ins with the

Pharisees. Matthew says that to Jesus, the people were like sheep without a shepherd. But Jesus had come to do something about that.

In the gospel of John, at roughly the same point in Jesus' ministry, we find the discourse on the Good Shepherd (chapter 10). Like the Matthean passage, it comes immediately after another conflict with the Pharisees, the false shepherds of Ezekiel 34 (see also Zechariah 11:17). Until now the focus has been the quality of the Good Shepherd, namely His listening attention and knowledge of the sheep. Here, in John's gospel, the focus shifts to the sheep and their one and only ability. According to Jesus, the sheep of His flock have one distinguishing characteristic: *They listen.*

> "The sheep listen to his [the Shepherd's] voice." (verse 3)
> "They know his voice." (verse 4, ESV)
> "They too will listen to my voice." (verse 16)

The ability of the sheep to recognize and respond to the shepherd's voice is the only characteristic they possess that keeps them alive. Jesus says they will run away from the stranger's voice (10:5). If they refuse to listen to their only Hope, they have no hope. Like the flock my friend encountered in the wilderness of Israel, Jesus' flock is a listening flock that recognizes the voice of the Shepherd.

> Give ear, O Shepherd of Israel,
>   you who lead Joseph like a flock!
>   (Psalm 80:1, ESV)

Lamenting:

The survival of the flock, based on the ability of the sheep to recognize and respond to the shepherd's voice, is grounded on a deeper and more secure truth — the existence of a *listening* Shepherd.

In Exodus 2 we read:

> During those many days the king of Egypt died, and the people of Israel groaned because of their slavery and cried out for help. Their cry for rescue from slavery came up to God. And God heard their groaning, and God remembered his covenant with Abraham, with

Isaac, and with Jacob. God saw the people of Israel — and God knew. (verses 23-25, ESV) (see also 3:7)

God's listening led to the eventual end of the captivity of Israel and their redemption. Like a shepherd, God would lead them to and through the wilderness. He would provide living water and manna to the hungering flock. Time and time again He would protect them from the predators who attacked. Whenever He heard the flock's bleating lament, He would move to shelter and defend them, even if it meant taking them first through the wilderness.

Though David would celebrate, "The LORD is my shepherd," in Psalm 23, the word "shepherd" is suspiciously wanting in the Psalter. In fact, it only appears twice, here and in Psalm 80:1. Perhaps this is because it is hard for the psalmist to conceive of a shepherd who would not listen, though the central hope in all the laments is to be heard by God (3:4; 6:9; 22:24; 66:19; 116:1). But with the coming of Jesus, the image of the Listening Shepherd became incarnate. The writer of Hebrews calls Him the "great Shepherd of the sheep" (13:20). His friend Peter refers to Him twice as the chief "Shepherd" (1 Peter 2:25; 5:4). We were like sheep, going astray, Peter says in 2:25.

Someone once told me that the best way to show people you love them is to listen to them. Listening is the flock's best way to love Jesus, the Good Shepherd. It is surely how He shows His love for us. It is also the way He demonstrates His love for the Father. In fact, if listening to the Shepherd is the defining characteristic of the flock of Jesus, Jesus' listening to the Father is what, in the end, qualified Him as the Good Shepherd. His Father's command was that He should lay His life down for the sheep (John 10:15-18). "This command I received from my Father," Jesus said. The Good Shepherd listened. He heard. He paid the painful price of perfect obedience.

For Discussion
1. Discuss what the phrase, "The LORD is my Shepherd," means to you now.
2. If we are called upon to be a listening flock, what is the Shepherd saying to us most often?

For Meditation

1. Take some time and repeat to yourself the Twenty-third Psalm. Understand yourself in the role of the listening sheep.

2. If the defining characteristic of the sheep is that they listen, what is the defining characteristic of the Shepherd?

19 | A Steadfast Stillness

The typhoon was not an exceptionally strong one, but it was massive, hundreds of miles across. It dumped several inches of rain on already soaked ground, and the annual flooding became even worse. It slammed into the eastern coast of China, the eye-wall brushing past the small village and the garage housing the underground Church where we were bound.

As a result of the storm, the plane we were supposed to catch was grounded. So we decided to make the long journey overland by means of a worn out, borrowed van. We finally arrived, twenty-four hours late, discovering to our amazement that the congregation of the small church had waited for us!

They had been singing songs through the night as they looked for us and waited. Their singing had attracted still more people. The original congregation of forty had grown to over six hundred, spilling out of the small garage and into the alleyway!

In almost any other situation, the pressure would have been unbearable — considering our lateness and the likelihood that we would not be able to deliver a message of music that would have been worth their extended period of waiting. Instead, I looked out on a sea of smiling faces. No sideways glances or rolling eyes. Our delay was unavoidable, a common part of their world — and so understood. We had come a long way simply to be together with them as our brothers and sisters. Again — understood.

A couple of us spoke our brief messages, punctuated by the crowd's "amens." We sang a few songs through a microphone plugged into an ancient record player. Too soon it was over, and we made our way out into the rain-soaked village.

The question foremost on my heart on this trip was, "What does lament look like in the persecuted Church?"

On the way out of the service, as everyone gathered their homemade wooden folding seats, an elderly woman in an impeccably clean, blue flowered blouse took me by the hand. She pressed it to her heart and through the translator said, "You don't have to leave. Why don't you just stay with us?"

Though most of her teeth were gone, her smile was radiant. She placed her gnarled hand on my head and we laughed together at my baldness. As we continued to walk along, she chattered away, leaving the translator far behind in the dust, repeating again and again her original invitation.

When we approached the van and it became clear that I was not free to stay and enjoy her hospitality, a calm settled over her that is impossible to describe. In the East there is an intuitive understanding of stillness which is rare in the West, but this was more than that. As she became still, her smile transformed. The deep wrinkles still formed the pattern of her smile, but her eyes, no less bright, looked away. I became aware that this was the moment I had come to China to experience. *This is the face of lament,* a voice inside my heart spoke.

I have had the privilege to know perhaps a dozen believers who have suffered for their faith. They have come from all walks of life, rich and poor, and from every corner of the world. Some are outgoing. Others more reserved. Some spoke my language, most did not. (Regrettably, I spoke none of theirs.) Yet they all had this in common, that same quality I sensed in the precious old woman who was forced to let me go. It is a steadfast stillness.

Grief resolved through lament becomes ballast, settling deep down in our souls. There, like the ballast in a ship, it "rights" us, keeps us upright in the midst of the typhoons. It is not an accomplishment earned by spiritual exercise but rather through simple acceptance of the Word that speaks, "Be still" (Mark 4:39).

The storms, the brokenness, the pain, the confusion, the disappointment that come when someone drops into your life for a few minutes and is then suddenly swept away — all these can be transformed, transfigured, calmed into a peace, into a stillness that is "righting" and steadying and steadfast. In the rain-soaked stillness that followed the typhoon, we had come together for a few precious hours. So many kind and encouraging words had been spoken, but most encouraging to me — of all that occurred on that memorable trip — was the stillness of the ancient countenance of my sister.

For Discussion

1. Discuss together the idea of "countenance" as a gift. Can you think of anyone who ministers to you simply through his or her countenance?

2. Paul makes the connection between suffering and perseverance in Romans 5:3. Can a further connection be made between perseverance and countenance? (see 2 Corinthians 4:6).

For Meditation

1. Spend some time meditating on Psalm 37:7, "Be still before the LORD and wait patiently for him" (see also 46:10; Zechariah 2:13).

2. Now spend some time in 1 Kings 19:11-13. Does God seem to use the contrast between noise and stillness to force us to listen and be still in the face of suffering?

20 | The Veil

Even when I am old and gray, do not forsake me, O God.
PSALM 71:18

My wife, Susan, and I wanted my mother to know that we had not forgotten her. When we finally built a house of our own, we included a bedroom on the ground floor with its own private bath. It would be a place just for her. From the beginning, we always assumed it was her room. But when the time came for her to move out of the big house she had stubbornly stayed in for too long, she refused to move in with us. "I would never do that to you," she repeated every time we would do our best to insist.

Instead, she moved into an assisted-living apartment close to her old neighborhood. Adamant about wanting her own space, she now had an apartment of her own with all the services she could ever want or need. She had lived with my father for fifty-three years, always caring for his needs and ours. Now she was on her own. A good situation, but still, to my mind, not the best.

When I visit her now, I pass through the lobby, where at any given time about half a dozen seniors, mostly women, wait by the door, waiting for their own families to visit or simply to see what's going on. I like to tease them on my way by. Most of them fire back, giving as good as they get.

My mother, who is ninety years old, appears at her door, always with a smile. I move from the busyness of my world into the simplicity of hers. Of all that the years have stolen from her, her sense of humor remains sharp as a razor. But around most of her other sensibilities a veil is slowly being drawn.

When we are very young — and again when we become very old — there is something I can only describe as a veil of innocence that surrounds us. Without the veil, the world would simply be too much for a young child to cope with. There are terrible knowledge and terrifying experiences from which the veil protects until we are old enough to begin to cope. The same holds true on the other side of life. Someone has called it the "second naiveté." The veil closes mercifully once more when we need to be protected again from the realities that would otherwise overwhelm and scare us to death. Without the veil, the end of life might seem more like a prison than a respite from all our labor.

My friends from China who have been in prison for their faith say that what caused them the most torment was not the physical torture they endured for their faith, it was the fear that they were forgotten by those on the outside. If you were to ask the ladies in the lobby what they fear most, my guess is they would not respond with medical complications, arthritis, or cancer. My guess is most of them would say what they fear, deep down behind the veil, is that they have been forgotten. Many of those who live with my mother — who see their cozy apartments as a comfortable prison — feel that way because they are forced to face the painful truth that some of their friends and families have indeed forgotten about them. This tends to tempt them to fear that God has forgotten about them as well.

Abraham Heschel once said that we exist as a thought in the mind of God. If He were to forget us, we would simply cease to exist. When our friends and families forget us, it is only natural to conclude the same thing about God.

In the very opening scene of 1 Kings, we catch a glimpse of the David of Psalm 71. He cannot keep himself warm at night, and so the beautiful Shunammite Abishag, comes simply to warm his bed and nothing else. It is not certain if David is completely aware of the power struggle that swirls around him, between Adonijah and Solomon. It is the last issue he must settle before he dies and "rests with his fathers."

In Psalm 71 the psalmist, most likely David, wrestled with the same fear that God might forget him in his old age. Like an older person repeating himself, David's opening plea occurs in two of his previous laments (25:2; 31:1). He cries out to the One who is his refuge, his rock, and his fortress. As his physical strength decreases, David is reminded every day of how much he needs the protection that only his Rock can provide.

In verse 9, mindful of his waning strength, he pleads for God not to cast him away in his old age. Once again, in verse 18 he echoes, "When I am old and gray, do not forsake me." As David nears death, it is not death he fears most but that his God might forget him.

How could the elderly king have forgotten the extravagant oath God Himself had made to him in Psalm 89:3-4? How could he have forgotten all the times the Lord had preserved and protected him? David needn't have worried about being forgotten, for though so much might have slipped his mind regarding his Rock, his Rock would never have forgotten him.

And so I sit with my mother as she wanders the pathways of her memories, amidst decades-old scenes so much sharper in her mind than what happened two minutes before. She worries about her memory sometimes. I am sure now and then she worries that we have forgotten her. But I can't help believing that what undergirds her good humor is the intuition that God could never forget. Even as He mercifully draws the veil around her for protection, His Son is preparing a place just for her.

For Discussion

1. Discuss the connection between the veil and innocence. Are they the same thing? Is one a manifestation of the other?

2. Decide on some practical ways to connect redemptively with just one senior.

For Meditation

1. Can you remember when you sensed the veil lifting from your life? For example, do you remember when your childhood innocence began to fade?

2. Take time to observe some young children. See if you can discern the veil.

Part Three

A Gathering of the Guilty

21 | The Man Who Would Not Weep

Then he went away and hanged himself.
MATTHEW 27:5

Before they apprehended his body, the heart of Jesus was first violently seized by that insidious kiss of Judas. With that treacherous act, the world started to turn in a dizzying way for them both. Everything is turned upside down, the innocent One is arrested, the Prince of Peace is engulfed in violence, Jesus is betrayed with a kiss — the tender betrayal of Judas. With this betrayal, the world will come crashing down for Judas, too. Whatever peace and clarity he might have known during the two and a half to three years he spent with Jesus will dissolve immediately as he leans in to give the familiar greeting of the most intimate friend.

A fairly good case can be made that up until the betrayal, Judas might have indeed been Jesus' closest friend. After all, he had been chosen as one of the Twelve and entrusted with the moneybag, not a responsibility Jesus would have given lightly. A reconstruction of the seating arrangement for the Last Supper indicates that, while John was sitting at Jesus' right hand, in the place of the honored guest, Judas was sitting at Jesus' left. In the ancient world this was known as "the place of the intimate friend." We're reminded of the psalm that says, "Even my close friend, whom I trusted, he who shared my bread, has lifted up his heel against me" (Psalm 41:9). Of course, this can only be speculation on our part, considering the fact that Jesus knew from the beginning what Judas would do (John 6:64; Mark 14:21), and realizing too that Jesus would have been incapable of a "false friendship." What then was their relationship like? Did Jesus simply take it a day at a time as He instructed His own followers to do? When the Gospels tell us that the disciples "returned with joy" after having been sent out on their first mission, would Judas have been a participant in that celebration? It doesn't seem likely that he simply lurked in the shadows all those months. What happens now, after the betrayal, is perfectly clear however.

Matthew tells us the burden of his guilt was simply more than Judas could bear. His world in fragments, he "went away and hanged himself."

Suicide is almost always motivated by despair. Kierkegaard described despair as the "sickness unto death." Despair, he said, is the sin that leads to all other sins. The prostitute sells her body because she despairs. The thief steals because deep inside, he has lost all hope. Judas despairs and hangs himself because he can see no other way to deal with the guilt and shame. With all Jesus had said about repentance and forgiveness, apparently Judas was unconvinced and could not imagine living with his sin. Neither it seems, could he imagine finding forgiveness from Jesus.

Of all the meaningless forms of violence, suicide is the most meaningless. There cannot be any meaning in the taking of one's own life, but only in the giving of one's life. That is the message of the Cross. In fact, the Cross of Jesus teaches us the only real meaning that can be found is in the giving of one's life. But Judas, it seems, could not or would not understand this. Apparently giving was not a part of his nature. His character is summed up in his question to the priests: "What will you give *me* if I hand him over to you?" Judas only wanted to take, even in regard to his own life. Jesus only wanted to give.

The cross of Christ and the gallows of Judas represent the extreme ends of the scale. Judas taking his own life was an act of supreme selfishness. Jesus dying on the cross was an expression of pure selflessness. Suicide is taking your life; the cross is giving your life. Judas died only for himself, Jesus died for us all. The person who commits suicide believes that by doing so they will stop the pain. The person who takes up the cross desires to absorb other people's pain.

The cross or the noose. Discipleship or suicide. One involves embracing life by taking up the cross of Jesus; the other tragically throws life away. The only way to really live is to embrace the Cross, the redemptive dying to which

Jesus calls all of his followers. Beside it, any other way is not only death but in fact is just another form of slow suicide, for damnation is a sentence of death that we pass upon ourselves by not following Jesus. Saying "no" to the Christ and the cross means saying "yes" to death and hell. If the One who was the Truth was telling the truth, then there is no other way.

Suicide, then, is motivated by the sin of despair; the cross of Jesus by pure love. "Greater love has no one than this, that one lay down his life for his friends," Jesus said (John 15:13). One of the friends for whom He laid down His life was Judas, whom He called "friend" even as Judas pursed his lips to kiss Him in betrayal. But Judas would have nothing of it.

In the end, there were two disciples who betrayed Jesus: Judas and Peter. Luke tells us that when Jesus' and Peter's eyes met across the courtyard at Caiaphas' house, Peter broke down and wept bitterly. At that moment, Peter realized that there was nothing he could do to "fix" things. All he could do was weep.

To the end, Judas was trying to undo what he had done. He tried to give the money back, but the priests would have none of it. In all the Gospels, there is not a word of Judas shedding a single tear.

For Discussion
1. Discuss the different ways Peter and Judas dealt with their denials.
2. What do Peter's tears tell us about how to handle our own betrayals?

For Meditation
1. In your imagination, contrast the way of the noose and the way of the cross.
2. What did Judas try to do with his despair that Peter did not try?

22 | Lessons from a Lesser Pain

Monday morning, 8:00. We were supposed to return the tour bus. Our agreement with the bus rental company says it must be cleaned before it comes back. Usually we simply pay someone else to do the job, but this tour left us without the funds to pay this fee. No one was free to do the job except me. And so, on what was supposed to be a writing day, I spent six hours washing the outside, cleaning carpets, laundering sheets, and making beds (twelve of them!), all the while muttering under my breath that I had something else more important to do! I finished around nine in the evening, exhausted and without the energy to write into the night.

As I lay in bed, grumpy, *irritated*, the Spirit started to teach the lesson. Did I think I was too important to do the job I was clearly being called to do? How often had I taught about humility? What about the life-changing lesson from my hero, Booker T. Washington, who spoke so much about the dignity of common labor?

God uses pain more than anything else to teach and shape us. One definition of "irritation" might be "a lesser pain." In my case, interruptions have become an extreme irritation for me. The succession of small hurts that continue to keep me from my "real" work are beginning to profoundly affect the way I see myself and those around me. This sort of severe schooling is what the Lord is best at.

Tuesday, 4:30 a.m. Once more, this was to be a day for writing, but then the phone rang. On the other end is the voice of the wife of one of my close friends. He is in the hospital. They are going into surgery in a couple of hours. Can I come and pray with them?

The whole of my spirit leaps at the chance. This is not an interruption, it is an opportunity to be with two people I love at a time when I might possibly be of some use to them. But as I'm driving into town, from a small, dark corner of my heart comes the self-centered voice whining, *But you were supposed to be writing* . . . This would not be so bad, but I answer with my own voice and in a huff say, "Well, yes, but . . ."

We sat together for about four deeply moving hours. We prayed and wept. We were simply *together*.

I returned home before noon with plenty of time left to write, but found that I was unable to do so. I was too burdened for my friend and his wife. What's more, I came home seeing my own wife in a new light. I couldn't leave her side for the rest of that day. The experience of the morning was too powerful a reminder of how precious she really is to me.

An extended time of prayer with loved ones; new eyes to see how precious the people the Lord has placed in my life really are — are these things not worth a few pages lost in my writing? The Spirit says, *Yes*.

Wednesday morning, 8:00. I fix breakfast. See the kids off to school. Come to my office. Start a fire. Turn on the computer, the entire day before me . . . The phone rings. It is the school nurse. My youngest son, Nate, has come into the school clinic complaining of a headache and sore throat. Can someone come and take him home?

The night before, Nate had rushed through a paper on Gettysburg. He had known about the deadline for days but had put it off till the last minute. On the way to fetch him, I began wondering if this might be a smoke screen. After all, what is easier to fake than a headache and sore throat? As I make my way into the office, my suspicions have grown to the point that I decide to confront him on the issue.

I speak to the nurse, then to the principal who calls Nate's room. I know better than to tell them about my suspicion. I don't want to betray my son. Still, I'm ready to come down hard on him if I find out he's been pretending.

Down the long hall I see his familiar silhouette limping along. As he comes closer the pallor of his cheeks is unmistakable. He is a very sick boy. I load him into the car and we make our way home.

In the quiet car, the hard questions are whispered by the Spirit once again: "What is really most important to you?"

"Can you not trust your own son?"

Lesson learned.

My mentor, Bill Lane, used to say, "Interruptions are my business." Only now does that lesson begin to really make sense.

The Lord is less interested in our gifts than He is in His own transformational work in our lives. If we have eyes to see it, He has a purpose and intention behind every interruption, no matter how irritating. In fact, the most irritating interruptions contain the promise of the most important lessons.

Family, friends, illness, hurts, needs, all these and more can become the sources of irritating interruptions. Through them God is nudging, whispering, His severe lesson — that loving and listening and trusting mean more than papers and books and deadlines. That even as He gives us first and foremost His presence, so we are called to be fully present for others in their suffering.

Jesus made the most of every one of the constant interruptions He faced. Yet He never once seemed irritated. Most of us are ready to admit, however reluctantly, that our painful experiences are used to teach and to draw us closer to God. What about the myriad lesser pains?

For Discussion
1. Share together some irritating interruptions from the past week.
2. Can you see any lessons to learn from them?

For Meditation
1. Think back on the life of Jesus. Do you remember times He was interrupted by the needs of those who were suffering? How did He respond?
2. Imagine, this very moment as you are trying to read and meditate with the aid of this book, that you are interrupted by what might seem an unimportant need from someone else. How might you respond differently now?

23 | Who Made the Man of Sorrows Sorry?

Who has believed our message? To whom will the LORD reveal his saving power? My servant grew up in the LORD's presence like a tender green shoot, sprouting from a root in dry and sterile ground. There was nothing beautiful or majestic about his appearance, nothing to attract us to him. He was despised and rejected — a man of sorrows, acquainted with bitterest grief.

ISAIAH 53:1-3, NLT

The cross loomed less than a week away. His feet still smelling of the perfume Mary lavished on them (John 12:3), Jesus entered Jerusalem for the next to the last time (Revelation 21:2). The large, ever-present crowd that always followed Him was there for the last time, too. Once the crucifixion would begin, they would disappear, the disciples first, fleeing in fear. John tells us that many had also come to see the *"dead man,"* Lazarus, who was walking into town beside Jesus (John 12:10,17). Entering Jerusalem in peace on a donkey, Jesus was coming to town with a resurrected man walking beside him.

Later, in a passage referred to as the "coming of the Greeks" in 12:20, we see one door closing as another opens. I believe Jesus clearly saw the coming of the Gentile Greeks as the sign for which He had been waiting all His life. From verse 23 on, Jesus' voice completely changes in tone. In verse 28, the Father will also speak one last time. From that point on, it is as if someone had switched on the countdown clock to the crucifixion. Rejected by His own people, sought out by the Greeks, Jesus will go to the cross and die for all of them.

"The time of judgment for the world has come" (John 12:31, NLT).

Shortly after saying this, Jesus will do something He rarely does; He will hide from the people (Mark 1:35; John 8:59).

From this point on, it is all about questions — asking the right ones and abandoning all the others that are empty and pointless. When John tried to sort out the mountain of disappointment and confusion, the Spirit led him to Isaiah, whom John says, "saw Jesus' glory and spoke about him" (John 12:41). At this point, before John needed the answer, he needed the right question. He found it in Isaiah 53:1. Isaiah's ancient question had become John's as well. Today, it must become ours.

"Who has believed our message?"

This is a crucial question for John. Perhaps it is the only question that really matters. How could it be, John must have wondered, that seeing was *not* believing? But Isaiah already had the answer to the question before John had even existed to ask it.

In chapter 53, Isaiah experiences the clearest vision of Jesus that I believe exists in the Bible. And, since none of the Gospel writers saw fit to actually describe Jesus for us, it is all the more precious. The prophet says Jesus was not attractive at all. There was nothing about Him that would cause you and me to take even a second look. In fact, He was despised and rejected, stricken, smitten, afflicted, crushed, wounded, oppressed, and cut off.

The question takes on a completely different tone when we come back to it after looking at Jesus through Isaiah's eyes, after seeing the wreck of the Messiah. Perhaps Isaiah should have asked, *"Who could possibly believe?"*

But tucked away in Isaiah's sad description is the only answer you will ever find to this question, which is the most important of all questions. The prophet says He took up *our* infirmities, carried *our* sorrows, was punished for *our* transgressions, and crushed for *our* iniquities.

Maybe now we are ready to try to answer that single, crucial question. Who has believed? The ones who see the wonders and miracles? (John 12:37). No. They will abandon Jesus every time. The only ones who truly believe this unbelievable message are those who come to realize that it was *their* infirmities, sorrows, transgressions, iniquities, and wounds that were taken up, experienced, and carried by Isaiah's unattractive Man of Sorrows. Jesus was sorrowful because we made Him sorry.

When the movie *The Passion* came out, the argument erupted all over: "Who killed Jesus?" The anti-Semitics blamed the Jews. The anti-Imperialists blamed the Romans. Socrates said that there are questions that set the mind turning vainly in circles. This is such a question. It is the wrong question to ask for two reasons.

First, the truth is, no one killed Jesus. The Gospels are clear that He "dismissed His spirit" (John 19:30). No one took Jesus' life, He let go of it voluntarily.

The second strike against the question "Who killed Jesus?" is, of course, the fact that we all killed Jesus. That is to say, our sins were the cause of His death. He died *for* them (Isaiah 53:10).

So Jesus is the Man of Sorrows precisely because *I* made Him sorry. As Rembrandt poignantly portrayed in his painting of the Crucifixion, I am the one who raised the cross. I drove the nails. If you want to find someone to blame for the death of Jesus, look in the mirror. The truth of this realization is not supposed to drive us away from Jesus. To the contrary, it should give us all the more reason to cling even closer to Him. Nothing will separate me from His love, not even my own sin that crucified Him.

The biblical response to this realization of our own sins wounding Jesus is called "contrition." In light of this painful knowledge, we become contrite. We lament the truth of our complicity. We lament the more painful truth that we tend to go on sinning, further driving the nails as it were, raising higher the cross. We sing of "lifting Jesus up," not realizing the darker truth behind that often-empty phrase. Perhaps it is time to stop lifting Him up in this way and turn instead to the lost language of lamenting our own sin. Only then will we be prepared to praise the One who suffered, died, and forgave them all.

For Discussion

1. Discuss as a group the loss of contrition in the church.
2. What are some ways we could bring about a renewal in this important area?

For Meditation

1. Do you remember the first time you felt the burden of your sin and took it to Jesus for forgiveness? What was that experience like for you?

2. How long has it been since you felt contrition for your sins since then?

24 | Beware Your Friends!

I am incensed at you and your two friends, for they have not spoken the truth about Me as did my servant Job.

JOB 42:7, JPS

They sit in a circle around a heap of ashes upon which their friend, Job, is sprawled. They have been silently weeping together for a solid week. Occasionally, Job's mind would wander out of the wilderness of his suffering and he would mutter, "Why, why, why?"

Altogether his friends somehow sensed that it was time to do something else besides weep — anything else! It was Eliphaz, the eldest friend, from Teman, a town well known as a seat of the wisdom school, who spoke first.

Job was startled by the sound of a human voice after so much silence. He opened his swollen eyes, gazing intently in the Temanite's direction. Inwardly he had been hoping all along that one of them might say something — some comforting words of understanding.

One of the most helpful pictures in the book of Job is the image of the "lamenter" who attempts to reach out to God but cannot get past the protests of his well-meaning friends. When you read the book with this perspective, it takes on a whole new meaning.

As the frustrating conversation begins between Job and his friends, as they parry back and forth between their theological condemnation and Job's righteous indignation, a subtle erosion begins to take place in Job's faith that bears mentioning.

When Job enters into his suffering, it is with a blessing for God on his lips (1:21). After his health falls apart, Job tells his condemning wife, "Shall we accept good from God, and not trouble?" (2:10). Anyone who has come to this place will tell you this is a costly understanding. To say in essence, "Whatever comes my way, I will not let go of God," reveals a heart that can accept suffering as the undecipherable mystery that it is.

But now, after their week of silence, the onslaught begins. Job will incessantly seek to cry out in lament to God, whom he will boldly address directly as "You" (7:17-21; 13:17 — 14:22). His friends will respond by insinuating that Job is suffering because of his sin and try to shush Job's lament due to their belief that such a conversation with God is blasphemy. This follows logically from their view of a God who is bound by the narrow equation of retribution. Would not such a God take vengeance on the arrogance of a person like Job who challenges Him to His face? Their God is a theological entity who sits on a throne. Job needs a God who will leave His throne and come to his rescue. That, they will all discover to their mutual amazement, is the God we meet in the book of Job.

"You subvert piety and restrain prayer to God," says Eliphaz (15:4). "That you could vent your anger on God and let such words come out of your mouth" (15:13; 34:36, JPS). But early on Job insists, "I will not speak with restraint. I will give voice to the anguish of my spirit. I will complain in the bitterness of my soul" (7:11). "I insist on arguing with God" (13:3, JPS).

Job desires to struggle in lament with God. He sees no other way out of the wilderness of his suffering, as indeed there is no other way out. His friends, who cringe at the apparent blasphemous passion of his language, shift the conversation subtly in another direction. They begin to talk *about* God. The Maker of the Universe is reduced to a subject they would have Job believe they understand. Their discussions *about* God incessantly break up Job's frustrated laments *to* God.

After Job's second lament (6:1 — 7:21), Bildad responds with the language of retributive justice, the old equation again. Job almost seems to be caught off guard and in 9:1-35 leaves his lament once more and begins to theologize against their narrow notion of how God works in the world. What is most significant is not the intellectual progress of their argument but the simple fact that Job is being distracted away from God. He does not return to lamenting to God until 10:1-22. Then Zophar appears, and the same process happens all over again. Before he returns to his important and difficult conversation with the Lord, Job has to reason with Zophar (12:1 — 13:16). Once again, he has stopped lamenting. God is slowly becoming merely a topic of theological discussion, no longer the One Job had been reaching out to so desperately.

Eventually, however, Job limps back to lament (13:17 — 14:22). It is here that Eliphaz pronounces the most forceful diatribe against Job's lamenting. At this moment, Job tragically gives up his lament altogether. From now on we hear only the lengthy responses from Job to their arguments (16:1 — 17:16; 19:1-29; 21:1-34; 23:1 — 24:25).

When he stops lamenting, Job abandons his reaching out to God. He stops worshiping, no longer able to see that only God is worthy to hear his case. What happened to Job happens to many of us who come to such desolate places, the extreme opposite of lament — despair. Kierkegaard rightly called despair "the sin that leads to all other sin."

Listen to the despair in Job's voice now as he moans, "Would that I knew how to reach Him" (23:3, JPS).

"He is not there" (23:8, JPS).

"He is hidden" (23:9, JPS).

"I am terrified in His presence" (23:15, JPS).

Not until 30:20 will Job attempt to cry out directly to God one last time. By then, everything seems to have changed. The fight has all but gone out of him. All he can mutter is, "I cry out to you, O God, but you do not answer."

Could it be that Satan, having seen that death and disease would not be enough to force Job to let go of God, sent Job's "friends" armed with an even more insidious weapon to attack him — cause for despair?

Job's distraction should serve as a serious warning to all of us. His friends were wrong about God. God Himself will say so (42:7-9). But Job was wrong as well. He was wrong to be distracted, to take his eyes off the God he could not see and focus them instead on his rationalizing friends. He was wrong to give up talking to God and resort to only talking about God. It was as close to the brink as Job ever came. But something seems to have held on to him in those last desperate minutes when he could no longer hold on for himself.

Job calls out to those of us who are in the wilderness, "Beware!" It could be that your undoing will not be caused by the death or the disease, by the cancer or the failed marriage. Your worst enemies could very well be disguised as your best friends.

This is how to know the difference. Your real friends will be willing to sit with you in silence — not for a week, but for as long as it takes. Your real friends will encourage you to keep talking, crying out to, and arguing with God. And when you would be tempted to despair and "quit the dance floor," saying that you simply lack the strength or the faith to go on, it is only your real friends who will have the love to leave you all alone with the One who desires, above all, to finish the dance with you.

For Discussion

1. What are the fundamental differences between talking to God and talking about God?

2. Where does loving advice fit into this scenario?

For Meditation

1. Trace in your imagination the journey of Job from chapter 1 to 42. Where does he begin and where does he end?

2. If his experience can rightly be characterized as a journey, what is the single element that best describes that journey?

25 | The Thorns That Won't Go Away

To keep me from becoming conceited because of these surpassingly great revelations, there was given me a thorn in my flesh, a messenger of Satan, to torment me. Three times I pleaded with the Lord to take it away from me. But he said to me, "My grace is sufficient for you, for my power is made perfect in weakness." Therefore I will boast all the more gladly about my weaknesses, so that Christ's power may rest on me. That is why, for Christ's sake, I delight in weaknesses, in insults, in hardships, in persecutions, in difficulties. For when I am weak, then I am strong.

2 CORINTHIANS 12:7-10

To the two most fervent prayers of lament in the New Testament, God answered "No." Both Jesus in the Garden of Gethsemane and Paul, here in his letter to Corinth, struggled with a God who sometimes refuses to deliver us from suffering. Whether it is the thorn in Paul's flesh, the thorns of Calvary, or our own sometimes thorny existence in this fallen world, often the suffering simply won't go away.

Corinth was a church in disarray. There was severe abuse within the congregation; some were even making personal attacks on Paul himself. When Timothy was sent to investigate the situation, he was treated with contempt (2 Corinthians 7:12). Paul had written a severe response, a "letter of tears," which has been lost (2 Corinthians 2:4). After the written rebuke delivered by Titus (2 Corinthians 7:5-8), the church repented and punished the abusers. As they were waiting for a follow-up visit from Paul, they received a letter from him. We know it as 2 Corinthians.

In the course of that letter the apostle was forced to defend himself. If you read between the lines, you can detect what some of the troublemakers had been saying about Paul. He had been accused of being vague and hard to understand (1:13), wishy-washy (1:12,15-17), frightening to the church (10:9), self-congratulatory (3:1; 4:2; 5:11,16; 6:4; 10:18), and restrictive of their freedom (6:11). They complained that he had been ungrateful by refusing to accept their financial support (11:7-11; 12:11-13), that he was crafty (12:16), and weak (10:1,10; 11:21,29; 13:3).

Paul displayed remarkable patience as he endured the barrage. As the smoke of the conflict settled, the church fought to regain its equilibrium. He realized that perhaps their attacks on him had come from a lack of vision for true leadership in the church. Paul had been living out a new and paradoxical portrayal of what an apostle of Christ should be and the Corinthian Christians had simply been unable to recognize it. The paradoxical new picture Paul presents in his letter is so thoroughly rooted in the life of Jesus you might take it for a portrait of Christ Himself.

A leader, says Paul, must embrace death for Jesus' sake in order to minister life to the church (2:14-17; 4:7-12). The first paradox: *Life comes from death.* The source of genuine wealth, he explains, comes from a leader's embrace of poverty (2 Corinthians 6:10; 8:9). The second paradox: *Riches come from poverty.*

The final piece of the new vision came by the disturbing means of an unanswered prayer — Paul's pleading prayer that the "thorn" be taken away. In 12:7-10, Paul hints at a magnificent vision he was granted fourteen years earlier. At the time he had only been a believer for about seven years. In this revelation, Paul found himself in paradise. There he heard "things" that he was not permitted to repeat. The result on his life was not spiritual superstardom or becoming elevated to the statue of "super apostle" (12:11). Instead, the effect on his life was devastating. What Paul can only describe as a "thorn" in his flesh was given to torment him, a "messenger of Satan."

Whatever the thorn was, Paul pleaded with God three times to take it away. The answer came back, "No." His temptation to become conceited for having been granted this "surpassing vision," would become the basis of his humility. The final paradox: *Strength comes from weakness.* Sometimes the thorns don't go away, and God has a purpose. When both Jesus and Paul experienced the "no" of God, they were faced with the same choices then that we still face today.

First, they might have concluded that God simply did not exist, that it had all been a lie; perhaps they had been deluded. This would be one explanation for why the thorns and the suffering of the cross did not go away. Perhaps there was no God to hear their plea in the first place.

Or they might have reasoned that God did exist but that He was not the God they had come to know from the Bible, that is, from His own revelation of Himself. This is the temptation many of the laments wrestle with, particularly the laments of Job. In the Scriptures, God has unequivocally revealed Himself as being infinitely compassionate, a God of *hesed*. If He continually ignores our pleas to take the thorns away, then He must not be the same God of whom the Bible speaks.

The next possible alternative would be to conclude that, for some reason, God was waiting to remove their suffering. He is indeed compassionate, but for some unknowable reason He was allowing the thorns for the time being. His ultimate intention is still to put an end to our pain; He will take the thorns away as soon as their purpose is fulfilled.

The puzzling silence of God is also one of the conclusions of the laments in the Bible. The lamenter wonders if perhaps the compassionate God is asleep or looking away for the moment. He only needs to cry loudly enough to awaken Him or else "tough it out" until the torment is over. At such moments, the cry inevitably becomes, "How long?" With intense suffering, this wait for relief can become unendurable.

The final possibility is based on a level of trust that is so radical it may seem almost paradoxical: Perhaps God's purpose is beyond our ability to determine or understand. Perhaps He is up to something completely apart from putting an end to pain. Perhaps even He uses pain to transform us. Or possibly even to save the world.

For Discussion

1. In what sense (to what degree) is God and the way He works in the world "knowable"?

2. What is the essence of the symbol by which that God is known?

For Meditation

1. When you read the list of accusations some of the believers were hurling at Paul, are you reminded of any time in your own experience when a group of people attacked their pastor?

2. There is a fundamental reality behind the perseverance involved in faithful suffering. What is it?

26 | In This Tent We Groan

Now we know that if the earthly tent we live in is destroyed, we have a building from God, an eternal house in heaven, not built by human hands. Meanwhile we groan, longing to be clothed with our heavenly dwelling, because when we are clothed, we will not be found naked. For while we are in this tent, we groan and are burdened, because we do not wish to be unclothed but to be clothed with our heavenly dwelling, so that what is mortal may be swallowed up by life.

2 CORINTHIANS 5:1-4

Five years ago, in the space of about a year's time, three of my closest friends died, all of cancer. The first was my precious nephew, Daniel, who had just celebrated his eighteenth birthday. He had patiently submitted to procedures and "last hope" cures over the course of almost three years. It was always two steps forward and three steps back. With a humble dignity that was almost transcendent, he bore the burden of his own disease as well as the weight we were all trying to carry for him. His simple submission to everything that came his way was the most powerful example of faith I have ever witnessed. He died, never even having had a girlfriend. He would have been the world's greatest husband and father.

From Daniel's quiet death I learned that what Abraham Joshua Heschel said was true: "For the pious man it is a privilege to die."[3]

The next friend who died of cancer was my mentor, William Lane. He had fought myeloma for months. I was holding his hand when he "fell asleep." He had called eighteen months earlier with the offer: "Let me come and show you how a Christian man dies." He did just that.

From him I learned a lesson contained in a phrase I heard him repeat again and again in our last months together: "This is a death-impregnated world."

The last to go was my friend John Eaves. His was stomach cancer. He had gone in for a routine physical and walked out with a six months prognosis. We had studied together with Bill Lane, calling ourselves by the proper German "Lane *schulers*." After school, John had first gone to the mission field, leaving behind a lucrative executive career in the oil industry. Next, he ministered to international students on the campuses of Harvard and Vanderbilt. We had watched Bill slip away together. After his own diagnosis, John mused that he had never thought he would be called upon to apply those lessons quite so soon.

"I am in the cancer club now," he would say with a genuine smile. "People will listen to me who would never listen to you." He didn't have to get cancer for that to be true. There were scores of people who always would rather have listened to John.

I was on the road when he died. I was on the road when they had his memorial service. We spoke on the phone the day before he died. He was worried about me.

From John I learned the lesson that the words of Jesus, "Take heart! I have overcome the world" were really true after all (John 16:33). I will always fear pain, but because of the way that John Eaves died, I will never fear death again.

Wonderful, costly, life-changing lessons. But to be completely honest, with a tear gathering in the corner of my eye, I confess I would rather the three of them were still here and I remain blissfully ignorant of those lessons. I have read a lot of comforting, biblical lessons about death and dying. None of them, not a single one, relieves my groaning. I miss my friends every day.

Paul, who might have actually been a tentmaker, spoke of our groaning in this earthly tent that is our body (2 Corinthians 5:1-2). He said we would be burdened with the desire to be clothed with a heavenly dwelling (see also 1 Corinthians 15:53). It is not the only time he spoke about this groaning (Romans 8:22). The truth is, Paul groans a lot in his letters.

If he were only a great theologian, Paul would have tackled the problem of suffering with theological formulae. He would have been a detached, theoretical observer. But Paul saw suffering as a present reality more than a problem to be solved. Like Jesus, he entered redemptively into the sufferings of the believers he encouraged. He entered redemptively into his own sufferings as well.

Before he died, Paul confessed to the church that suffering was the source of his strength. I wonder if, after he was gone, they wouldn't have still rather had the passionate little bald-headed Jew present with them, sans the lesson.

Too often his letter to the Romans is regarded merely as a theological work. This is a cunning scheme that evades the heart-changing missionary character of the letter. In verses three to five of chapter 5, Paul gives one of the "chain sayings" that he and his friend Simon Peter must have loved to use in their sermons (2 Peter 1:5-7).

The chain begins with suffering. Paul then proceeds up the chain with a short list of single-word lessons. If we could only learn to rejoice in our sufferings, he says, these lessons might be ours. The two central links in the chain are perseverance and character, costly lessons that on most days you and I would just as soon remain ignorant of. The chain ends in hope — not a solution to suffering, not a fix or a cure, not even in the promise of the end of suffering, just hope.

If we dared to be honest with Paul or ourselves or God, we might mutter that we were hoping for a little more than just hope as we huddle in our worn-out, earthly, cancer-ridden, death-impregnated tents. But as he so often does, Paul anticipates our response.

"Hope does not disappoint us," he counters, because God has poured something into these hearts that beat so feebly behind the worn-out flaps of our earthly tent. He has poured His *love* into them through His Holy Spirit (Romans 5:5).

I read those words in the full stature of my skepticism, with pictures of three wonderful men smiling back at me, men who died in pain and too early. I reach way back into the reservoir of my own hurt for a cynical dismissive response and I find . . . nothing. I am not disappointed — me, the most sinful, spoiled, skeptic in the whole bunch. I try to breathe in the truth of the realization, but it takes my breath away. (Truth always does.)

Hope — and a heart filled with a love that has come to me from beyond the walls of the world. The presence of a Spirit that is truly holy, dwelling here with me, within my ribs, within the tatters of my earthly tent, ready, when the time comes, to groan for me with words I cannot find in myself to utter.

For Discussion

1. Discuss together the prospect of your own deaths. In your circle of family and friends, what lessons will you leave behind?

2 Critics might label Paul's words about the hope of a heavenly dwelling as "pie in the sky." What makes that kind of statement untrue?

For Meditation

1. Write your own obituary.

2. Imagine the world, your world, without you in it. Who would be the most affected by your homegoing? What could you say to them now to make things more meaningful?

27 | All I Have Left

The sacrifices of God are a broken spirit;
a broken and contrite heart,
O God, you will not despise.

PSALM 51:17

I n the ancient world, those who worshiped pagan gods lived in constant fear and darkness. The gods were perpetually angry and malevolent. They needed to be continually appeased, most often with human blood.

The followers of Baal used to cut themselves with stones (1 Kings 18:28). The worship of Molech involved throwing innocent infants into a sacrificial fire that had been kindled in the bronze belly of the idol (2 Kings 23:10; Jeremiah 7:31). The Philistines worshiped their god, Dagon, the god of war, by offering the severed head of Saul in their temple near Gilboa (1 Chronicles 10:10). It is only to be expected that unholy pagan gods, made by men in man's image, would be just as bloodthirsty as their creators.

In the Old Testament, the God of Abraham never asked to be appeased. Though sacrifice was a part of His worship, the character of those offerings was completely different. The purpose of sacrifice to Him was not appeasement but atonement.

When David brought the ark of the covenant back to Jerusalem, it is said that every six steps along the way he sacrificed a bull as well as a fatted calf. All the while, he danced before the Lord, half naked, like a madman (2 Samuel 6). He was clearly not motivated by fear, but rather uncontainable joy. The presence of the Lord, represented by the ark, had returned to his people. In order to properly cleanse the way for his holy God, he joyfully had sacrifices made. David's God was not angry; He was holy. David's dancing joy came because he was confident his sins were being atoned for.

Even when David sinned with Bathsheba, recorded just five chapters later in 2 Samuel 11, there is no word of anger from the Lord toward David. The Bible says that what David did *displeased* the Lord. If the Lord had been like the pagan gods, David would have to do something to make things right once more.

But when you read David's lament for his sin with Bathsheba closely, you'll notice there is not a hint of fear. It is God's kindness (*hesed*) that has broken David so completely and brought him to this level of repentance (Romans 2:4). He has come to realize the unbearable burden of his sin before God. He has seen, perhaps for the first time, that there is nothing he can do to make this right again. His only hope is the compassionate mercy of the Lord. God must blot out his transgression (Psalm 51:1), wash and cleanse him (verses 2,7), blot out his iniquity (verse 9), create a clean heart in him, and renew a right spirit (verse 10), restore the joy of his salvation and sustain him with a willing spirit (verse 12). No river of blood, no herd of bulls or fatted calves slaughtered every six steps, can atone for his sin (Hebrews 9:11-14). God must do what He did for Abraham on mount Moriah, what He did for us on Calvary's mount; God must provide the sacrifice.

But there is still an offering to be made on David's part — the only thing he has left. It is not the fatally beating heart of an innocent lamb he needs to offer, but his own broken heart; not the innocent spirit of a spotless dove, but his own contrite spirit.

Though most of us would not admit it, we live as if our God was always angry and in need of appeasement. We spend our lives trying to sacrifice enough to make things right — enough hours of the day, enough good works, enough worship songs. This was van Gogh's painful struggle. But it is only in lament, when we see that all we have left is all God ever wanted in the first place, that we come to the end of appeasement and begin to celebrate the true worth of God. The atoning sacrifice that His holiness required could have only been offered by Himself — in the sacrifice of Himself. The motivation was not anger but holiness. On Calvary He was not appeased, He was satisfied.

For Discussion

1. Be completely honest with each other: Who still lives their lives in order to appease God, so that He will not get angry?

2. I've heard Brennan Manning repeatedly say, "If you don't have to be afraid of God, you don't have to be afraid of anything." Discuss this together in light of Proverbs 1:7.

For Meditation

1. Read Proverbs 1:7. Does this statement give rise to a natural question?

2. Given what we have learned about the journey of lament, a journey outlined in the Wisdom section of the Old Testament, what is the end of wisdom?

28 | The Power of Memory

I remembered God.
Psalm 77:3, kjv

James, the younger brother of Jesus, was fascinated by a peculiar image, an image that parabolically points out one of our most fundamental flaws. In James 1:23-24, James paints an intriguing image of a man who looks at himself in a mirror and walks away, forgetting what his own face looked like. James employs this haunting parable to illustrate a person who hears the Word but then does not respond in obedience by putting it into practice. James recognized that there is a regrettable link between disobedience and forgetting, but there's a promising connection between redemption and remembering.

Perhaps the brother of Jesus, who was so thoroughly immersed in the Old Testament, had Deuteronomy 4:9 in mind when he told the sad story of the man who forgot his face:

> Only be careful, and watch yourselves closely so that you do not forget the things your eyes have seen or let them slip from your heart as long as you live. (see also 8:11)

Reminding us of what we already know is one of the basic purposes of the Scriptures; over and over the Bible encourages, warns, and woos us not to forget (Deuteronomy 4:23; 6:12; 32:18; 1 Samuel 12:9; 2 Kings 17:38; Psalms 9:17; 50:22; Isaiah 51:13). Story after story speaks to us of those who did forget and the tragic consequences. Helping us not to forget is one of the main reasons the Bible exists; otherwise, we would read it once and be done with it. But the truth is, the Bible is never done with us.

The biblical laments recognize our fundamental flaw of forgetfulness. They recognize that forgetting cannot only be a cause of disobedience; it can also become a reason to lose hope — just as remembering can become an occasion for finding it again. In the laments we frequently see the forgetful lamenter, who is tempted to give up hope, looking back to remember what God has done in the past and finding there a new hope for the present. The laments testify to this hope-giving power of memory by means of a literary device called the "formula of remembrance."

> These things I remember
>   as I pour out my soul:
> how I used to go with the multitude,
>   leading the procession to the house of God,
> with shouts of joy and thanksgiving
>   among the festive throng.
>   (Psalm 42:4)

> When you went out before your people, O God,
>   when you marched through the wasteland, *Selah*
> the earth shook,
>   the heavens poured down rain,
> before God, the One of Sinai,
>   before God, the God of Israel.
> You gave abundant showers, O God;
>   you refreshed your weary inheritance.
> Your people settled in it,
>   and from your bounty, O God, you provided for the poor.
>   (Psalm 68:7-10)

> But you, O God, are my king from of old;
>   you bring salvation upon the earth.
> It was you who split open the sea by your power;
>   you broke the heads of the monster in the waters.

It was you who crushed the heads of Leviathan
>   and gave him as food to the creatures of the desert.
It was you who opened up springs and streams;
>   you dried up the ever flowing rivers.
The day is yours, and yours also the night;
>   you established the sun and moon.
It was you who set all the boundaries of the earth;
>   you made both summer and winter.
>   (Psalm 74:12-17)

We will not hide them from their children;
>   we will tell the next generation
the praiseworthy deeds of the LORD,
>   his power, and the wonders he has done.
He decreed statutes for Jacob
>   and established the law in Israel,
which he commanded our forefathers
>   to teach their children,
so the next generation would know them,
>   even the children yet to be born,
and they in turn would tell their children.
Then they would put their trust in God
>   and would not forget his deeds
>   but would keep his commands.
They would not be like their forefathers —
>   a stubborn and rebellious generation,
whose hearts were not loyal to God,
>   whose spirits were not faithful to him.
>   (Psalm 78:4-8) (*What follows is sixty-three more verses of remembering the great things the Lord had done!*)

The power of memory is not that it somehow creates hope by itself, but rather it provides a means of connection to the only One who can provide hope. When the future seems to hold only fear, the past can become a source of real hope. When, in the present moment, the presence of God seems impossibly absent, remembering those times in the past when His presence was palpably real can make today's suffering more bearable.

In the parable of the man who forgot his face, it is you and me, of course, who walked away from the mirror, because we will always be prone to forget. But even more remarkable than forgetting the image of your own face, which changes every moment with shadows and with time, is to forget the face of the One who gave us our faces, to forget all His "benefits." What unforgettable things has He done in your life that are worth remembering? Remembering them is the first step back toward not forgetting Him. And if you are in a painful place right now, where even the burden of remembering is more than you can bear, remember: He has not forgotten you.

> Can a mother forget the baby at her breast
> and have no compassion on the child she has borne?
> Though she may forget,
> I will not forget you!
> See, I have engraved you on the palms of my hands.
> (Isaiah 49:15-16)

For Discussion
1. Discuss together some of the chief things God has done in your life that are worth remembering.
2. What is the source of forgetfulness? Ingratitude? Fallenness?

For Meditation
1. Take as much time as it requires to remember God's presence in your life, the first moment you became aware of it.
2. Read Psalm 78 and look for parallels to your own experience with God.

29 | The Gulf Between Faith and Correctness

Surely I spoke of things I did not understand,
things too wonderful for me to know. . . .
Therefore I despise myself
and repent in dust and ashes.

JOB 42:3,6

My youngest son, Nathan, is one of the most tenderhearted people I have ever known. He possesses a set of emotional antennae that draw him automatically to the most hurting person in any crowd. At the same time, he also has a wonderful mind. He enjoys deep discussions about topics like truth and the nature of God. I know he is my son, but I have never known anyone like him.

However, his unusually perceptive concern for the hearts of other people, combined with a remarkable intuition, frequently presents him with a problem. In any given situation, he will know what he needs or wants to say, but his concern for others will keep him from saying it. Recently, Nathan wanted something from the store, but knowing that money was tight at the moment, he did not ask for it. In fact, when I asked, he denied wanting it. He felt that to say what he wanted would be "wrong." So he opted for saying what was "correct," not what was faithful to his heart at the moment. It is a struggle I hope he comes to understand more clearly as he grows up.

Lament teaches us that sometimes there is a gulf between faith and "correctness." Sometimes faithfulness demands a transparency from us that requires us to say things that, strictly speaking, are not correct. But the God who is as intensely concerned with our hearts as with our minds encourages such honest conversations. He wants us to tell him how we are feeling as much as what we are thinking — especially when we are tempted to think that what we are feeling may be "incorrect."

Job probably said more incorrect things to God than all the other characters in the Bible combined. Yet, even with all his untruths, God seems to have been incredibly fond of him; in fact, He boasted that He had never known anyone like his "son" Job (Job 1:8; 2:3; 42:8).

But still Job became acquainted with all our grief a thousand years before the Man of Sorrows wept. Everything a person can lose, he lost: his possessions, his health, the respect of his wife and friends, and most gut-wrenchingly, his children. He suffered at the hands of terrorists, the Sabeans and the Chaldeans, who killed his servants. He was forced to defend his own innocence before his friends, who should have known and trusted him better. He sits on the ash heap, surrounded by his companions, the loneliest man in the Old Testament. As he wrestles with God in lament, many of the things he says are profoundly untrue. Some of these untruths must have broken the heart of the God who loved him so dearly. Listen to the disturbingly incorrect voice of a man who nonetheless remains faithful to God:

> The arrows of the Almighty are in me . . .
>   God's terrors are marshaled against me." (Job 6:4, JPS)

> If I have sinned, what have I done to you,
>   O watcher of men? Why have you made me your target?
>   (7:20, JPS)

> Even if I summoned him and he responded,
>   I do not believe he would give me a hearing. (9:16, JPS)

> Does it please you to oppress me . . .,
>   while you smile on the schemes of the wicked? (10:3, JPS)

> Turn away from me so I can have a moment's joy. (10:20, JPS)

You destroy man's hope. (14:19, JPS)

God assails me and tears me in his anger
    and gnashes his teeth at me. (16:9, JPS)

God has turned me over to evil men
    and thrown me into the clutches of the wicked.
    All was well with me, but he shattered me;
    he seized me by the neck and crushed me.
    He has made me his target;
    his archers surround me.
    Without pity, he pierces my kidneys
    and spills my gall on the ground.
    Again and again he bursts upon me;
    he rushes at me like a warrior. (16:11-14, JPS)

God has wronged me. (19:6, JPS)

He tears me down on every side till I am gone;
    he uproots my hope like a tree. (19:10, JPS)

Again and again Job's friends remind him just how incorrect it is to speak to God in such ways (8:1; 11:2-3; 15:2-5). But Job rails back that he will not keep silent; he will speak; he will complain (7:11).

When it is all over and everyone has had his say, God tells Job's friends that He is angry with them. "You have not spoken of me what is right, as my servant Job has," he says (42:7). This is a remarkable statement, given the catalog of errors that have just flowed from Job's angry lips.

Job refused to say what he thought God wanted to hear. Even at the risk of his life, as an act of faith, he became completely transparent and told God exactly what was in his heart. It was not "correct" but it was true. In the end the apology does come. "I spoke of things I did not understand, things too wonderful for me to know. . . . I despise myself and repent in dust and ashes" (42:3,6). Job is sorry for the things he said, but they still had to be spoken. They have become a part of God's perfect Word.

As we struggle in our search for the hidden face of God, lament encourages us to never give up, to never quit the conversation. We may kick and scream if we must, and when we don't have the words, the Bible will provide them. But never, never, never let go of God. Never walk away.

For Discussion

1. As a group, can you come up with anything that should never be said to God?

2. Job's well-meaning friends were acting out of the best of motives when they tried to shut him up. Can you think of times when you spoke to a friend something you should have kept to yourself, especially something that was "correct."

For Meditation

1. Look into your heart and ask if there is anything you have wanted to say to God but have always been afraid to say. Now, say it.

2. Look back through the book of Job and track the progression of the dialogue between Job and his friends. Take note of the times Job quits lamenting to God and begins talking about God. See if you can get a feel for the emotional progression in Job's experience.

Part Four

The Man of Sorrows

30 | The Disturbing Faithfulness of God

And I am sure that God, who began the good work within you,
will continue his work until it is finally finished on that day
when Christ Jesus comes back again.

PHILIPPIANS 1:6, NLT

In one of his most recent books, Walter Brueggemann prays, "You are not the God we would have chosen."[4] The troubling truth of that prayer resonates in my heart. It sounds a distressing, self-evident reality that I would evade if only it were possible. But there is no escaping the sometimes-disappointing otherness of God. The truth is, most often, I would have chosen (and indeed go on choosing) a god other than Him. Most often, I would rather not be forced to do it His way and always learn the hard lessons the hard way. I would rather not have to worship in the wilderness, where He continually calls me to find and be found by Him. I would rather God simply meet my expectations, fix my problems, heal my hurts. And I think you would, too.

As we enter more deeply into a real, biblical relationship with the God of Scripture, we increasingly discover to our great annoyance that, despite the reports of so many American Christians, most often God simply refuses to answer our prayers our way. We plead for healing, yet the cancer rate among Christians remains virtually the same as those outside the faith. But isn't Psalm 103:3 crystal clear? He "heals *all* my diseases." We respectfully request some financial help; after all, Philippians 4:19 explicitly promises "God will meet *all* your needs according to his glorious riches in Christ Jesus" (my italics). The pat response usually goes something like, "You must not have enough faith." But clearly Jesus said faith is not a matter of quantity (Matthew 17:20; Luke 17:6). So what is the missing piece of the puzzle? If answering my prayers my way is not the shape of His faithfulness, then what is God's faithfulness supposed to look like?

This is surely the question that troubled Job. The religious world he inhabited believed God's faithfulness should always look like doing, fixing, judging, (even cursing), answering, and healing. That, at least, was the point of view of Job's friends. In return for works-righteousness, they believed that God was obliged to make things right for His people. But Job, whom God Himself declared righteous, is beset with every sort of suffering and loss. A thousand years before the Man of Sorrows, Job became acquainted with all our grief. In return for his righteousness, Job received unimaginable suffering. Where was God's faithfulness? As you spend more and more time in the book of Job, you begin to wonder if the deepest source of his pain was not the slaughtered children or his wrecked health, but rather the terrifying prospect that the true God might indeed be nothing like the god of his equation.

In Job's world, God was a question-answering god. But when the God of Job finally appears, He only asks more questions. How disappointing for Job's friends. The god of Job's world was a judging, condemning god. But the God behind the real story clearly has more in mind than sentencing and punishing. His faithfulness is expressed in a way that no one could have ever imagined. *He showed up!* Nothing could have been more disturbing for the lot of them.

"I had heard about You," stammers Job, "but now my eye sees You" (42:5, NASB).

A God whose faithfulness is made visible simply by showing up . . . sound familiar?

In His own time, as well as ours, everyone who came close to Jesus was disappointed by His disturbing revelation of just what the faithfulness of God was like. There were those who wanted Jesus to judge and condemn. In John chapter 8, the scribes and Pharisees hounded Jesus for a judgment against the woman who was caught in the act of adultery. If He was faithful to their notion of God and the law, they reasoned, Jesus had no other choice. After all, she was caught in the act. But Jesus refused to condemn her because, as Frederick Buechner once said, "He would be condemned for her" (Luke 12:14; Matthew 7:1).

"I pass judgment on no one," Jesus will say in verse 15 of John 8. Later, in the face of their disbelief, He declared, "I did not come to judge the world, but to save it" (John 12:47). Jesus' disturbing faithfulness does not appear in the shape of condemnation. Instead He *showed up* (was Incarnate) to save!

Others wanted healing, and certainly Jesus healed them by the thousands. But faithfulness for Jesus didn't always look like healing. In John 11, after hearing of the life-threatening illness of one of His closest friends, Jesus appears to loiter where He was for two more frustrating days. As a result, Lazarus dies. Martha and Mary appear with the same disappointed accusation on their lips, (though I believe in two completely different tones of voice). "If you had only been here, my brother would not have died," they say. If only you had fixed things, healed him, answered our prayers the way we wanted them answered. But, like His Father, Jesus has come to show us that God is faithful to us in ways we could have never dreamed. Before Jesus moves on to the tomb of His friend, to call the "dead man" from the grave, He enacts what most of us never regard as a miracle. But it may be the most miraculous miracle of the whole story. The miracle? Jesus wept. He *showed up* and entered fully and painfully into the suffering of his friends.

Who is God for you? The Answer Man? The Fixer? Is He the theological Entity, frozen on the throne? Is your greatest hope for Him that He might appear someday and pass judgment on your enemies? Or could He possibly, unimaginably be the God we meet in Job, who descends from the throne room where He has been dealing with the accusations of Satan, and shows up, having been moved there by Job's tears.

Who is Jesus for you? The great Teacher? The miracle worker? Is He merely the caricature of American Christianity, walking three inches off the ground? Is your greatest hope for Him that someday He will appear and judge all those other denominations "guilty"? Or might He impossibly be the very image of the God whose disturbing faithfulness to us looks like Incarnation, like simply showing up; showing up to make His name "Immanuel" true in the fullest way it could ever be true; showing up, not to wave the magic wand, but to enter into our sufferings "with us." Could it possibly be true that the greater miracle is not the healing or the unexpected check that saves from bankruptcy, but the unthinkable truth that God has chosen to be with us through it all? Could it possibly be true that the miracle is not provision, but Presence?

It is time we begin to understand the real reason for what seems to be the inexplicable rarity of God's intervention in the ways we expect Him to act. Is it not time that we begin to wonder if perhaps He is up to something else, if He is not working a more miraculous miracle than we could ever imagine? Is it not time for us to see that His not giving the answer we ask for has a deeper purpose? He, the God of the Universe, has determined to do a work in (not for) us. Paul declares in Philippians 1:6 that He has promised to complete this interior, spiritual work until He is finally finished, and that will be on the day Jesus *shows up* fully, finally, and completely, once and for all time.

In our frustration we cry out to the heavens. We shake our fists at the sky, demanding that He act, move, fix, heal. We insist that God be faithful according to our expectations of what faithfulness should look like. We who have exhibited so little faithfulness in our own lives have the audacity to believe we know what it should look like for Him. My mentor, Dr. William Lane, used to say, "We want the God of the magic wand. The God who makes the cancer go away. But more remarkably, He is the God who comes alongside us and suffers with us. He is the God who never leaves us."

Ask yourself, how did God Himself speak of His faithfulness? What are the words He most often used in both the Old and New Testaments to describe what it would look like? How about:

"Never will I leave you; never will I forsake you." (Deuteronomy 31:6; Hebrews 13:5)

or

"Now the dwelling of God is with men, and he will live with them." (Exodus 25:8; Revelation 21:3)

Faithfulness resembles most the One who showed up and, in the process, became acquainted with all our sorrows. His promise of faithfulness is heard in His parting words, "Surely I am *with you* always, to the very end of the age" (Matthew 28:20, emphasis added). It is the best promise any bridegroom can possibly make to his bride.

But still, Brueggemann is right. He is not the God we would have chosen, but neither could we have dreamed up nor imagined such a God — a God the immediacy of whose Presence is incarnate in us by His indwelling Spirit, a God who is committed to the throes of completing this labor of indwelling us, of being born in and through us. It is His deepest desire. It is the greatest of all His wordless miracles and yet we are unsatisfied with Him and want more. He is not the God any of us would have chosen but, as Brueggemann marvelously concludes, He is the God who has chosen us.

For Discussion

1. Discuss openly and honestly your true expectations of God.

2. Before you read this reflection, how would you have responded to someone close to you who was suffering?

For Meditation

1. In your imagination, contrast and compare the images of the "American prosperity god" with the God of the Bible. Once you see them clearly in your mind, honestly ask which one you would choose, if you did the choosing.

2. Think back to your most recent experience of a prayer that seemed to go unanswered. In light of this reflection, ask yourself what else God might have been doing in your life.

31 | The Laments for Jerusalem

"O Jerusalem, Jerusalem, you who kill the prophets and stone those sent to you, how often I have longed to gather your children together, as a hen gathers her chicks under her wings, but you were not willing! Look, your house is left to you desolate. I tell you, you will not see me again until you say, 'Blessed is he who comes in the name of the Lord.'"

LUKE 13:34-35

As he approached Jerusalem and saw the city, he wept over it and said, "If you, even you, had only known on this day what would bring you peace — but now it is hidden from your eyes. The days will come upon you when your enemies will build an embankment against you and encircle you and hem you in on every side. They will dash you to the ground, you and the children within your walls. They will not leave one stone on another, because you did not recognize the time of God's coming to you."

LUKE 19:41-44

Mary, the daughter of Eleazar, was from the village of Bathezor (the "House of Hyssop"). She was from a family that had prospered on the other side of the Jordan. So when, late in AD 69, word reached their village that the Roman commander Titus and the tenth Roman legion were on their way to lay siege to Jerusalem, she and all her relatives fled to the illusion of the protection of the city walls with only the possessions she could carry. Once the legions had surrounded the city, Jewish partisan chiefs along with their bodyguards plundered what little she had left, leaving her and her infant son destitute. She cursed the looters, screaming at them to kill her out of anger or pity. Later, when the partisans returned, to their horror they discovered that she had murdered the baby and was roasting him over a fire. "Eat," she told them with a ghastly stare, "for I also have eaten." Josephus said the battle-hardened chiefs went away trembling (*The Jewish Wars* 6.194-213) (Matthew 24:19-21).

Josephus says that during the siege of Jerusalem mothers snatched food from the hands of their starving babies. He speaks of men who devised unspeakable tortures for those who had hidden food. As the siege neared its end in the sweltering month of August, bodies were piled high in the narrow alleyways. Josephus says there was no weeping or wailing as "hunger conquered emotion, and those who were dying looked with dry eyes on those already dead. A lethal darkness shrouded the city" (*The Jewish Wars* 5:512). When Titus later surveyed the heaps of bodies, he raised his hands and called out to God to bear witness that this was not of his doing (*The Jewish Wars* 5:519). Josephus estimated the toll at somewhere just over a million. More than seventy thousand were sold into slavery.

Some forty years before, when Jesus saw Mary in His mind, His eyes were not dry. Tormented by what He knew the daughter of Eleazar would do, He trembled in horror at the thought of it as He entered the city for His last time amidst confused cries of "Hosanna." He saw the bodies and heard the wailing echoing from the future. He felt the eerie ache of the black silence that Josephus says eventually settled over the city.

Jesus laments twice for Jerusalem in the gospel of Luke (Luke 13:34; 19:41-44). The first account occurs at some point along the final journey to Jerusalem. The second lament happens when Jesus comes over a rise in the road and sees the expanse of the city. Matthew 23:37 echoes precisely the words of Jesus' first lament in Luke 13. It is safe to assume that this represents yet a third lament, after He had entered the city for the last time (Matthew 21:1). It was a song, the words of which Jesus could sadly repeat by heart. In this twice-recorded lament, He quotes a line from Psalm 118, another lament which speaks initially of being surrounded by the nations and of being cut off on every side. This is a glimpse into the mind of Jesus as He entered

Jerusalem in what is wrongly called the "triumphal" entry. Having lamented for Jerusalem at least three times that we know of, they mistook Jesus for Jeremiah, the weeping prophet (Matthew 16:14).

Not long ago I stood beside what is left of those walls. The enormous pile of rubble the Roman soldiers pushed over the walls when they destroyed the Temple in AD 70 is still there. Not one stone was left on another, precisely as Jesus had said.

Imagine it is September 10, 2001, and you find yourself standing outside the World Trade Center. In a flash of prophetic insight, you suddenly see in horrifying detail precisely what is going to happen in just twenty-four hours. What would you do?

Would you take a cab to FBI headquarters and try to find someone who would believe your incredible story of the imminent disaster? Do you think anyone would listen to you? And if that failed, would you hurry back to the WTC's lobby and plead with everyone coming and going to stay away from work tomorrow? When that didn't work would you frantically go banging, door to door, pleading with anyone who would listen?

Completely exhausted, you might just collapse into a chair in the lobby, having realized how hopeless it all is. What then? Unless you have no feeling heart, my guess is you'd do just what Jesus did when He topped that rise outside the city and saw Jerusalem for the last time. You would lament. You would lament that something was coming about which you could do nothing but weep.

For Discussion

1. The laments over Jerusalem seem not to have been heard in the midst of the crowds. There is no word of anyone responding to Jesus' lament. Why do you think this is so?

2. Jesus, who clearly sees what will happen to the Holy City in the near future, chooses to weep rather than warn. What possible effect could His tears have had?

For Meditation

1. Read and meditate upon Psalm 118. The psalm celebrates the love (*hesed*) of the Lord enduring forever, yet it is set in the midst of a siege. Is a time of struggle when we truly experience the truth of this psalm?

2. The psalm contains a prophecy in verse 22 concerning the "stone the builders reject." Both Jesus and Peter understand this verse in relation to Jesus' rejection (Matthew 21:42; Mark 12:10-12; 1 Peter 2:7). Is the confidence of Peter and Jesus rooted in the tone of this psalm, which celebrates victory in the midst of what seems total defeat?

32 | A Questionable Sorrow

You will grieve, but your grief will turn to joy.

JOHN 16:20

In Judaism, they are called the *Shelosh Relagim*, the "big three." They were the required pilgrimage festivals, that is. If you lived within twenty miles of Jerusalem, you were required to come to the Temple and celebrate them (Exodus 23:14).

Pesach, or Passover, was the biggest. That festival celebrates the time the angel of death "passed over" everyone who had the blood of the lamb marking the doorposts of their homes (Exodus 12). The climax of this celebration is the Day of Atonement.

Sukkoth, or Tabernacles, was next, a festival based on remembering the time when the children of Israel wandered in the wilderness for two periods or forty years, living in "booths" or *Sukkoth*. It was celebrated during the harvest. We have Americanized it into Thanksgiving. The connection is that workers in the field lived in huts or booths during this season. For this reason, it is also known as the "Feast of the In-gathering."

The third was Pentecost, or *Shabuoth*, also known as the Festival of Weeks. It is a time for remembering when Moses gave the Law and the people were consecrated by God as a "holy people." In the synagogue, the book of Ruth is read aloud on this day.

Jesus said in Matthew 5:17 that he had come to "fulfill the law." He had come to offer once and for all the sacrifice for sin required by the Law to make atonement. When you consider the fact that the *Shelosh Relagim* are also included in the law, a good case can be made that Jesus also perfectly fulfilled the meeting of the big three feasts.

Tabernacles, the Feast of the In-gathering, will be actualized at some unknown future time, yet it has already been "fulfilled" in Jesus. In Revelation, the second coming of Christ is pictured as a harvest (14:15). The Angels will wield harvesting sickles as the "wheat" is gathered and separated from the "weeds" (Matthew 13:24-30,36-43).

Pentecost was fulfilled by the coming of the Spirit in Acts 2. The disciples had waited in Jerusalem for fifty days (*pente kostus)*, having been told to do so by Jesus. On the Day of Pentecost, the Holy Spirit came, flickering over the heads of the followers of Jesus as tongues of fire. In effect the Spirit's coming signified that every believer had become a living tabernacle, since the pillar of fire over the tabernacle in the wilderness signified God's presence within. God was consecrating a people once again, and all that Pentecost might have meant, it now did mean, because of the coming of Jesus.

Of all the three, the biggest of the big three feasts was Passover. The central focus of the feast was the Passover lamb. The New Testament reminds us that Jesus is our Passover Lamb (1 Corinthians 5:7). He was crucified precisely during the time when the lambs were slaughtered in the Temple (3-6 p.m.). None of His bones were broken, a mandate given for offering the lamb (Exodus 12:46; John 19:31-36). Because of His sacrificial death, the angel that is the second death will "pass-over" those of us who have marked the doorpost of our hearts with His blood. Every facet of the Law was perfectly fulfilled in Jesus, including the symbolism of the three great feasts.

In Judaism, the celebration of Passover is a time of joy. But when Jesus fulfilled this great feast of joy, He also transformed it into a day of lament, a sorrow made all the more sorrowful by the church's ironic title "*Good* Friday."

The Friday we call "good" was the day He died for us, was tormented and tortured, suffered the punishment that should have been ours. Historically, the church has mourned the whole of this day. In fact, the entire season of Lent, leading up to Passover, is devoted to contrite solemnity. Statuary in the church are draped in black. And it is forbidden to speak the word "hallelujah." But most churches in our culture no longer celebrate the Friday we call "good" with these sorts of meaningful tokens of observance.

In one sense it is not hard to understand why the American church has departed from this tradition. Isn't a day of mourning uncalled for; after all, isn't Easter coming? Is this not a questionable sorrow? Wouldn't we just be pretending? Wouldn't we seem insincere?

This point of view exposes the misunderstanding of lament that lies at the heart of the modern church. It reveals how our fear and refusal to enter into redemptive sorrow has robbed us of the true meaning and joy of Easter. It exposes the fact that we have forgotten that *suffering is a door.*

On the Friday we call "good," we are called to gather around a crucifix and open the eyes of our hearts to gaze intently on the suffering of which we were the cause. We are invited to stand together with all believers in Jesus and claim our solidarity with a crucified man who is the Savior of the world, to take His suffering seriously, not skipping over it in order to land untouched on Easter Morning to gather candy eggs. We are called to come, beckoned by all those who first stood before that original Roman cross, to stand on the blood-soaked ground and lament the utter absurdity of it all. For only here is where the true meaning of it all is founded: that life only comes from death, that the seed must die, that sorrow is the prelude to deep joy, that every hope, every dream must die in order for the dream of a new hope to be truly born.

The weeping women and John and Peter whisper in our ears what they experienced that horrific evening when all their hopes died. Mary Magdalene leans in to us, covers her face, and sobs, "it was all for nothing!" She forces us to realize that we will never understand the joy of Easter, until we experience along with them the death of all our hopes and dreams that occurs on the Friday we call "good." To stand before that cross with them is to realize that at that point nothing seemed more likely than the fact that Jesus' life had all been for nothing. When Jesus said, "It is finished," they heard, "It is over." This complete destruction of hope explains why the next morning the women came to anoint a *dead* body, not to wait expectantly beside a tomb for the resurrection Jesus had so clearly promised. This explains why, even when they saw the resurrected Jesus, they mistook Him for someone else. Their dreams had to be totally destroyed so they could be completely reborn. All things had to be made new, their hopes as well as their hearts, their dreams as well as their souls. It must all be made new. Before they could taste perfect joy, they had to drink fully from a cup of sorrow.

This is why we are called to enter into the questionable sorrow of the Friday we call "good." This is why Jesus bids us to enter through the door of lament, so that our joy may be full, so that then and only then will it become so deeply rooted in our hearts and in reality that no one will be able to take it away from us, ever!

For Discussion

1. How is it possible to truly experience the sorrow of Good Friday when all along we know that victory is coming with the dawn?

2. Discuss together the impact of meal fellowship and the ritual observance of Passover on the Christian community in regard to recapturing the meaning of Easter. Have you ever experienced a Passover seder?

For Meditation

1. Take a few moments to read back through the Passion narratives. Use your imagination to place yourself at the foot of the cross. If you had been present all along the way with the disciples and the watching women, would you have come to any different conclusions?

2. Now read a few of the post-resurrection appearances. Given the bleak experience of the day before, can you understand their joy in a fresh way?

33 | The Lonely God of the Garden

My soul is overwhelmed with sorrow to the point of death.
MATTHEW 26:38; MARK 14:34

The overwhelmed soul of Jesus . . . *unimaginable!*

All along the final journey to Jerusalem, Luke paints a picture of a Jesus who is becoming more and more isolated and alone (Luke 9:51 — 19:28). Through the course of his narrative, John uses a literary device, the motif of misunderstanding, to slowly separate Jesus, the Wisdom of God, from the foolish misunderstanding of men. Every time he says something deeply spiritual, the response of the hearers reveals the fact that they simply cannot comprehend this increasingly lonely man (John 2:20; 3:4; 4:11; 6:28; 7:35; 8:19; 11:24; 12:28-31; 13:36; 14:5; 16:17). Mark, who records the testimony of Simon Peter, portrays the close personal friendship between Jesus and Simon rapidly eroding once they reach Jerusalem for the final week. Once they come to the garden, hours before the courtyard at Caiaphas' house, Peter has already begun to think to himself, *I don't know this man.*

By the time the Eleven reach the gate to the estate of Gethsemane after the final supper, they are all exhausted and confused by the troubling pronouncements of Jesus during the past few hours. On their long walk from Jerusalem out to the Mount of Olives, Jesus had told them they would all desert Him that evening (Mark 14:27). Jesus posts the eight at the entrance. He moves farther into the darkness of the olive grove with the three. "Stay here and keep watch," He charges Peter, James, and John; but they prove to be supremely incompetent lookouts. Jesus wanders off alone into the shadows of Gethsemane, the "Place of Crushing." Just after they left the eight, Jesus confided in Peter, James, and John that His soul was becoming so mournful that He felt He was about to die.

The word the Gospels use for "soul" is *pseuche*. It can be variously translated, life, breath, or soul. Another way to render the verse might be, "My life is so overwhelmed by lament that I am about to die." Jesus had promised that, as the Good Shepherd, He would lay down His *pseuche* for his sheep (John 10:11). In Matthew 20:28 He promised to give His *pseuche* as a ransom for many. Earlier, in 10:39, Jesus promised His disciples that if they would only lose their *pseuche* they would find it. If what He said about losing in order to find and dying in order to live was really true after all, Jesus was about to find His *pseuche*.

Peter remembered Him falling on His face there in the garden under the weight of His overwhelmed soul. Three times Jesus stumbles off into the shadows to pray by Himself. Each time His prayers seem to grow in intensity until, during the final painful session, the sweat on Jesus' face becomes drops of blood. During this final, most intense period of prayer, Luke says an angel appeared to comfort Jesus (22:43). But apparently even the presence of an angel had no effect of comforting Him. What Jesus needed most is what, at that moment, seemed farthest away (Psalm 69:3).

It is a real human being who leads His disciples into the lonely garden. He isn't walking six inches off the ground. His feet feel every sharp stone. His pain is real, perhaps the most untainted pain that was ever experienced. His struggle is genuine. If you do not understand that in the garden Jesus was thoroughly tempted to say "no" for the first time to the Father, you do not understand what happened in Gethsemane. In essence Jesus is saying, "If there is any way out of this, *I want out*." That is the intention of the words, "Let this cup pass."

Once you begin to understand the scope of the struggle, you will start to appreciate the scale of Jesus' suffering. The earth must have rumbled as He whispered, out of breath, "Not what I want, but *what You want*." These were the costliest words that were ever spoken by the lips of any man. The costliest and the most precious, for they made possible the purchase of the salvation of the world.

But where is the response of God? None of the Gospels record a single word. The answer to the most impassioned plea of the Son of God was the silence of God.

God spoke audibly at least three times in the life of Jesus: at the baptism (Matthew 3:16-17), at the "coming of the Greeks" (John 12:28), and at the Transfiguration (Matthew 17:5). In both instances in Matthew God says, "*This is my Son.*" The words are addressed to the witnesses, not directly to Jesus. (Luke and Mark agree with Matthew on the wording at the Transfiguration but not at the baptism.) In John, at the coming of the Greeks, in response to Jesus' prayer "Father, glorify your name," God says, "I have glorified it, and will glorify it again." But Jesus' explanation of the Father's words to the crowd hint that perhaps, even here, God was not talking to Him. "This voice was for you, *not for my sake,*" Jesus says.

These incidents hint at something that is both extremely sad and also wonderfully encouraging at the same time. Perhaps Jesus, *even Jesus,* lived His life, as we all do, within the context of the silence of God.

We usually imagine Jesus' prayer sessions as times of "sweet communion." But perhaps more often they were like the time of bloody sweat in the Garden of Gethsemane. Perhaps this garden prayer was more representative of His entire prayer life. I must say that this thought brings a certain sadness, to think that still another part of Jesus' suffering for me was that in His Incarnation, He chose to be silently cut off from God in the same way that you and I are cut off. And yet at the same time, it fills me with a hope that is beyond words, that Jesus, *even Jesus,* in experiencing every part of humanity (except for sin) knew what it was like to call out to the Father and hear only the silence of God in response! If this is true, you and I are not — and cannot be — alone in this frustrating experience ever again. It means that every time we suffer the silence of God, it is an occasion to be brought closer to Jesus. It means that He has chosen to join us in that silence and fill it with His understanding Presence.

For Discussion

1. Recount together the events of the last night of the Passion of Jesus. As a group, discuss the subtle erosion of relationships that led to the disciples abandoning Jesus in the garden.

2. Discuss together why we as a culture are so uncomfortable with silence. Could it be because silence says too much?

For Meditation

1. How does your soul respond to the idea that Jesus might have spent His life within the context of the silence of God?

2. Is God's presence any less real when it is wrapped in silence?

34 | Isaiah's Unimaginable Image

He was despised and rejected by men,
a man of sorrows, and familiar with suffering.
Like one from whom men hide their faces
he was despised, and we esteemed him not.
Surely he took up our infirmities
and carried our sorrows,
yet we considered him stricken by God,
smitten by him, and afflicted.
But he was pierced for our transgressions,
he was crushed for our iniquities;
the punishment that brought us peace was upon him,
and by his wounds we are healed.

ISAIAH 53:3-5

The pages of the Old Testament are haunted by a person who kept His name a secret (Genesis 32:29; Judges 13:17) and was wounded. Zechariah encounters him in a vision and asks, "What are those wounds on your body?" To which the mysterious man answers, "The wounds I was given at the house of my friends" (Zechariah 13:6). Of course, you and I know His name as well as why He was wounded.

Isaiah gives the most vivid picture of Him of all the prophets. In chapter 53, he sees the same wounds that Zechariah saw. He notices as well that the man is sorrowful, perhaps he was weeping. But Isaiah seems to better understand why the scars and the tears are there. He opens his disturbing prophecy about the wounded Messiah with a perfectly natural question: "Who has believed our message?" (53:1).

Certainly no one in Jesus' day was willing to believe in a weeping and wounded Redeemer. The Jews were looking for a Messiah who would come and rule an earthly kingdom. But when they tried to make Jesus king by force, He ran away (John 6:15). The Samaritans called him *Tahav*, "the revealer." Though the Samaritan woman at the well recognized the One who revealed her life, by and large the Samaritans rejected Jesus (Luke 9:51-53). The Zealots believed in a warrior Messiah who would kill the Romans. Though perhaps at least three of Jesus' disciples had been Zealots, by and large He must have been a disappointment to the party. After all, Jesus did not come to kill the Romans, but to die for them. The Pharisees were only ready to believe in a paragon of purity. Jesus perfectly obeyed God's law, but disappointed them at every turn—sometimes deliberately breaking their oral laws of purity. Every day most of the Jewish men who eventually rejected Jesus prayed these words, later recorded in the Talmud as the Twelfth Article of Faith:

> I believe with complete faith that the Messiah will come and although he may tarry, yet each day I will wait for his coming. (Talmud, Sanhedrin, 10)

The Pharisees taught that "He who when he prays, does not pray for the coming of the Messiah, has not prayed at all" (see John 1:48). How is it then, with all these expectant prayers, that so many people missed it? Who has believed?

After the Resurrection this question becomes even more frustrating as, again and again, Jesus' own followers fail to believe and recognize what has happened to Him.

In John 20:15, Mary mistook Jesus for the gardener. She had come with absolutely no expectations of witnessing the resurrection. She only came to anoint a dead body. When she saw that the stone had been rolled away, it was not a sign to her that Jesus' words about rising from the dead had come true. She assumed the obvious, that someone had simply stolen the body. It was only when Jesus spoke her name that Mary recognized Him by His voice.

The disciples on the road to Emmaus, in Luke 24:13-32, walked and talked with Jesus for hours, long enough for Him to explain everything in the Old Testament concerning Himself. Amazingly, they failed to recognize Jesus as well. It is not until later in the evening, when Jesus broke the bread, that their eyes were opened and they recognized Him.

Finally, in John 21, at the second miraculous catch of fish, we read a mysterious verse (verse 12). "None of the disciples dared ask him, 'Who are you?' They knew it was the Lord." They knew because Jesus had repeated the miracle from Luke chapter 5. But somehow, too, they did not know. John's curious statement is an echo of Zechariah's query to the mysterious wounded man. It is a mystery that perhaps we will never grasp. The Gospels do not explain this mystery, because apparently they don't think we need to know. Who has believed? Had Mary, or the disciples?

One thing is absolutely certain. When Jesus wanted them to recognize Him, He pointed to His scars. Even before the doubting Thomas incident, the Bible says, "He showed them his hands and side" (John 20:20). Jesus is recognized by His woundedness. It has always been and will always be that way.

In Revelation, Jesus is referred to as "the Lamb that was slain from the foundation of the world" (13:8, KJV). When John was standing in the middle of the multitude and one of the elders shouted, "Look, the Lion of the tribe of Judah," he looked up, expecting to see a lion. Instead John sees a lamb. And how does he know who that Lamb is? He recognizes the wounds (Revelation 5:5-6).

The scars were allowed to remain on Jesus' otherwise perfect resurrection body. He would be recognized by them. They were His identifying mark, not His brown eyes or the freckle on His cheek. Jesus was recognized by the scars He had incurred on the cross. Like every other paradoxical piece of His story, those brutal scars are a part of His glory.

The question still resonates, "Who has believed?" Who has believed in this unbelievable Messiah? Who has recognized Him by the wounds He received for His friends? Who is ready to follow the One who is known by His scars? Who will respond to the call of the Man of Sorrows, who bids us to weep with those who weep? Who has believed? It is still, after all those centuries, the only question that matters.

For Discussion

1. Is the image of a wounded Messiah any more palatable today than it was in the first century?

2. The followers of Jesus failed to recognize Him after the resurrection because they had no expectations of seeing Him. How does this relate to us today and our failure to perceive what Jesus is doing all around us?

For Meditation

1. Meditate on the image of the wounded One who shadows the pages of the Old Testament. Ask yourself why His name was kept secret.

2. What is the effect of the simplicity of the question, "Who has believed?" Does it make the question harder to evade?

35 | A Blessing for Those Who Weep

Blessed are you who weep now,
for you will laugh.
LUKE 6:21

What I needed to hear most today, I did not hear. At the funeral of my uncle, I stood outside on a perfect fall day, next to his open grave. Gathered there were his elderly friends, many of whom could barely walk the uneven ground to the graveside. We had not been close. He was a doctor and was always busy at the hospital whenever we had family get-togethers. Not getting to know him was just one of many regrets that were on my heart.

My uncle was being buried next to his father, my grandfather, whom I also never knew. They were both "Dr. Fred Brown." He a doctor of medicine and my grandfather a doctor of theology. And now their gravestones stand side by side with the same name. Unfortunately, they had never gotten to know each other either. My grandfather, being the pastor of a big and busy church, was always somewhere else. Later in life he told one of my aunts that not getting to know his only son was his biggest regret.

When I close my eyes, I can smell the pine tree next to the graves. It makes me remember the times we used to come and play here in the graveyard, finding my grandfather's headstone among the sea of headstones. That was forty years ago. I have played far too little in the years since then. I added that to my list of regrets.

This graveyard was the first place I ever experienced holiness. My grandfather was revered by the family. Whenever we shared a meal, the conversation would eventually come around to him. Though he had been gone for decades, it was as if he were still a part of our coming together, so powerful was his personality, even all those years later. We would come here as children to be as close to what was left of him as we could. I remember tracing his name on the cool tombstone:

Fred F. Brown

A servant of Jesus Christ

Nov. 27 1882

Aug. 9 1960

Such experiences with holiness have been few and far between in the intervening years. I regret that too.

As the unbearable weight of all these misgivings and more began to press down on me, as they compressed my soul, I began to weep. Just at that moment the memorial service began. I waited to hear those words I so badly needed to hear another human voice speak, but they were never said. I needed to hear *Jesus'* words, not pointless poems, not even the kind words that were being spoken about my deceased uncle. I felt as if I were standing on one side of a river I badly needed to cross and only the hearing of those words would get me over. I needed to hear, "Blessed are you who weep . . ."

The pronouncement of blessings (*barochim*) was a very rabbinic thing to do. We see Jesus as a rabbi being asked to give His *barocha* to children, to lay His hands on them and pronounce a blessing that often had a prophetic character.

There were many prescribed blessings in Judaism. When wine was tasted the blessing was, "Praise art Thou, Eternal, our God, king of the world, who has created the fruit of the vine." Upon seeing a wise man the blessing was, "Praise art Thou, Eternal, our God, king of the world, who has given from his wisdom to mortals." Whenever you encountered someone who was handicapped, you were supposed to bless them with these words, "Praise art Thou, Eternal, our God, king of the world, who produced variously formed creatures." There were proscribed blessings to say when you saw a rainbow, when you received good news or bad news, when you smelled sweet-scented wood or oil or spices; a blessing for every imaginable occasion. (Perhaps it is time to recover a tradition of blessing.)

In Luke 6, Jesus pronounced a disturbing list of blessings no one had ever heard before. No one had ever thought of blessing the poor, since their poverty was thought to be a curse from God. The same could be said for the other unlikely recipients of Jesus' radical *barochim*. Having just called the Twelve, He was just beginning to reveal to them the unexpected shape of His kingdom. Each of those blessings spoke of the kind of radical reversal that would become part and parcel of being His future followers—that true Wisdom would only be found by fools, that only a child can become fully mature, that true prosperity is only to be found in poverty.

In the middle of this remarkable list, Jesus' blessing falls on those who weep, for often those who weep feel cut off, even sometimes cursed by God, as if they were on the other side of an uncrossable stream. In Jesus' kingdom such will not be the case; that stream will be crossed by a bridge of lament called into being by Jesus' blessing. It is a bridge made out of our tears and His. Those who weep will be called to cross over, from despair to hope. Of all that "blessed" can mean, this is the most profound blessedness.

Those who weep are blessed because they recognize the depth of their sin and allow their hearts to be broken by it. Their tears are a testimony to the painful honesty that confession demands, just as they are a tangible proof of the overflowing joy of knowing His forgiveness. Jesus' blessing is an encouragement to offer God what He wants most from us: our broken hearts and contrite spirits (Psalm 51). Those who weep are blessed because it is only in the hopelessness of tears that they will discover their last hope is their only hope.

As the memorial service comes to an end, I help my mother walk to the waiting car. She is telling me stories about Fred as a little boy, how once, when he was carrying two large buckets of water from the spring, he tripped on the doorstep and spilled both of them. The cold spring water dripped through the floorboards, soaking her as she slept downstairs. After he cleaned up the mess, he fetched two more buckets and tripped again in exactly the same place! She wipes the tears from her eyes as she tells the story. She is almost ninety, and I sense in her few regrets.

I am still hungering to hear those five simple words of Jesus: "Blessed are you who weep." I need to know just now that I am indeed blessed, in spite of all my regrets, in spite of all my failures as my mother's son, in spite of all my sins. Perhaps there are more tears that need to be wept before I am ready to really hear them.

For Discussion

1. Discuss together some of the unique possibilities offered by a funeral.

2. Share together your first experience of holiness.

For Meditation

1. Think of a few of your deepest regrets. Decide to act on those it is not too late to do something about.

2. Reread the blessings of Jesus. Try to imagine them being spoken directly to you by inserting your name in the text.

36 | The God-forsaken God: Part 1

The Seven Last Words

The magnitude of the moment of the Cross in universal history cannot be overstated. Everything in Jesus' life led up to it. The Cross was the reason He was born in poverty, amid the laments of Rachel weeping for her children. The experience of His entire life of becoming acquainted with our deepest sorrows was simply the prelude to this moment. The fundamental proof of His incarnation, along with His blood, was His tears. When the Man of Sorrows was being most used by God, He was lamenting.

There are seven excruciating pieces of this final puzzle, the last words of Jesus from the cross. You will notice that they are all short, gasping phrases. You must understand that in order to utter them, Jesus had to push up on the nails in His feet in order to draw a shallow breath. Once each of these seven statements was made, the full weight of His body fell back onto the nail in His hands. These seven last words make up the final lament of Jesus.

> 1. When they came to the place called The Skull, there they crucified him, along with the criminals — one on his right, the other on his left. Jesus said, "Father, forgive them, for they do not know what they are doing." (Luke 23:33-34)

Luke, whose collection of eyewitness accounts of the Crucifixion contain more of the words of Jesus than any of the other Gospels, tells us that when they came to the place of the Skull (*Golguloth* is the Hebrew word for skull, hence Golgotha; *Calvaria* is the Latin for skull, hence Calvary), "there they crucified him." All of the Gospels are equally wanting for details of this actual moment. There is no word of His hands and feet being nailed there. That detail comes prophetically from Psalm 22:16. In the Gospels the only indication we have that Jesus was nailed to the cross are those post-resurrection appearances when He points out the scars to His disciples.

His first word from the cross is "Father." As He enters into His suffering, this word will disappear as an excruciating indication of His torment.

"Forgive them," Jesus says, "They don't know what they are doing." His final lament begins with the theme of forgiveness. His enemies are stretching out His arms on the crossbeam, nailing seven-inch Roman nails through the flesh. He had told the disciples to love and forgive their enemies. "God is kind to the ungrateful and the wicked," one of the most extraordinary phrases to have come from a life of extraordinary sayings. In manifest kindness, Jesus genuinely asks for the Father to forgive, absolve, the three Roman legionaries who will execute Him.

> 2. When Jesus saw his mother there, and the disciple whom he loved standing nearby, he said to his mother, "Dear woman, here is your son," and to the disciple, "Here is your mother." (John 19:26-27)

John, who was the only disciple spoken of as having actually been present (though I am convinced Simon Peter remained somewhere close by), takes up the story of Jesus' final words. We know that Mary was there, along with a group of women who will become the definitive witnesses of the Crucifixion and Resurrection. Luke tells us that they had been the source of financial support for the three-year time Jesus was on the road. From the beginning they had always been there. Now, at the end, nothing could have kept them away.

Being the oldest son, Jesus would have been responsible for the care of His mother. If anything had happened to Him, the responsibility would have fallen to the next oldest male child, presumably James. It is curious, then, that Jesus entrusts His mother to John, the youngest of the disciples. We are told that she went to live in his home from that time on. Tradition says John was with her when she died.

In the garden, amidst the tremendous struggle of will Jesus was caught up in, three times He broke off His prayers to come and check on the three, worried that they might be falling into temptation. Now, here at the cross as Jesus faces the struggle of His life, He is nevertheless mindful of His mother. Though His lament comes from the deepest part of the self, it is not selfish or self-centered. He is concerned for the soldiers. He is concerned for His mother. And perhaps this second statement shows a measure of concern for the youthful John, who may have, at this point in his life, needed Mary more than she needed him.

3. Then he said, "Jesus, remember me when you come into your kingdom." Jesus answered him, "I tell you the truth, today you will be with me in paradise." (Luke 23:42-43)

We return to Luke for the third word of Jesus from the cross. At first both of the thieves had been cursing Jesus along with the crowd, "heaping abuses on him." But something has moved in the heart of one of the criminals. Most certainly it was something that Jesus said, perhaps the kindness of Jesus' plea for forgiveness for the soldiers. Acknowledging his own guilt, this one thief now seeks forgiveness for himself.

He has learned Jesus' name and calls him by it. He is one of the few people in the Gospels who will address Jesus simply by His first name. Notice that he does not ask specifically for forgiveness. He asks to be remembered. In effect, the repentant criminal is voicing what so many other lamenters in the Old Testament expressed: We exist as a thought in the mind of God. To be forgotten by Him is to cease to be. To be remembered is salvation.

Jesus' response is literally, "Amen to you, I say today with me, you will be in paradise." The longest phrase Jesus utters from the cross, it is a promise of paradise. Paradise is the oldest word we know of. It retains its original consonantal form in a variety of ancient languages, *prds,* to the very beginnings of language. It is the word for garden.

Lament began in a garden. The promise of Jesus to another crucified man is that he will awaken with Him in the garden that he — that we all — are created to inhabit.

For Discussion

1. Why should it be that the Gospels provide so few details of the crucifixion of Jesus?

2. Discuss together the implications of the promise of the Garden Paradise made to the thief on the cross.

For Meditation

1. During the life of Jesus, the continuity of His relationship with the Father was unbroken, except for one moment.

2. How do you respond to the statement, "When the Man of Sorrows was being used by God the most, He was lamenting"?

37 | The God-forsaken God: Part 2

The Seven Last Words
4. At the sixth hour darkness came over the whole land until the ninth hour.
And at the ninth hour Jesus cried out in a loud voice, "Eloi, Eloi, lama
sabachthani?" — which means, "My God, my God,
why have you forsaken me?"

MARK 15:33-34

As Jesus enters into the darkness of the hidden face of God, as He begins to experience that separation which is hell itself, the pain can be most acutely felt by the disappearance of the term "father." He has become now "God," but still *my* God.

Jesus knew as He entered the Passion that the disciples would forsake Him (Matthew 26:31). While certainly a source of pain and discouragement, this probably came as no surprise to Him. But when Jesus utters this fourth wailing cry, it almost seems as if His abandonment has come as a disappointing surprise. After all, they had been one for all time, from eternity. Now, for the only time in eternity, that unity was impossibly broken. Jesus has become sin (2 Corinthians 5:21). The Father must look away (Habakkuk 1:13). The horror expressed in a hundred laments in the psalms, the terror of being forsaken by God, belongs to Jesus alone. He is the God-forsaken God.

If lament is a bridge of tears, it is also a bridge of hope. On the cross Jesus is clearly crossing this bridge. He finds the words He needs to stay connected to the Father in the words of David's lament in Psalm 22:1. The hope that will sustain Him through the rest of the ordeal he finds in verse 24:

> For he has not despised or disdained
>> the suffering of the afflicted one;
> he has not hidden his face from him
>> but has listened to his cry for help.

5. Later, knowing that all was now completed, and so that the Scripture would be fulfilled, Jesus said, "I am thirsty." (John 19:28)

On the way to the cross, Jesus was offered a stupefying drink by the pious women of Jerusalem to dull the pain (Matthew 27:34). Jesus tasted the drink, but then refused it. He would not allow the pain to be lessened by drugs. Now that He has reappeared from the darkness, John says Jesus deliberately makes this statement in order to fulfill a prophecy, Psalm 69:21.

His encounter with the woman at the well must have seemed an eternity ago to Jesus. On that sweltering afternoon He had promised her that if she received the water He was offering, she would never be thirsty again.

But now He is thirsty.

In a time when fresh, clean water was more scarce than wine, the soldiers were given sour wine to drink when they were in the field. This vinegar is offered to Jesus from a filthy sponge. The fact that the soaked sponge had to be placed on a long stalk to be lifted to his lips indicates that Jesus was crucified on a high cross.

Like His abandonment of the term "father," the fact that Jesus asks for a drink hints at the ordeal He has just endured. So to fulfill a prophecy from another lament (which also pleads for God not to hide His face), Jesus drinks sour vinegar from a soiled sponge. It would seem that this was more a matter of obedience than an act that would actually quench His thirst.

6. When he had received the drink, Jesus said, "It is finished." With that, he bowed his head and gave up his spirit. (John 19:30)

John, who actually witnessed the final drink from the sponge, tells us that immediately afterward Jesus literally said, "It has been completed." That is, all that the Father had required of Him, everything to the smallest detail, had been perfectly, obediently endured. The One who drank from the foul sponge had also drained the cup of suffering dry. The experience, from which He had pleaded in the garden to be spared, was now completely finished. Jesus was done.

One of the greatest temptations we face when we are struggling in lament before the Father is to lose hope by believing it is never going to end, that whatever it is we are suffering will simply go on forever. Jesus' sixth word of lament from the cross teaches otherwise. There is an end to suffering and tears. It is a solemn promise that comes more than once in the Scriptures. For now, as we are called to bear our individual crosses, there is no greater source of hope than the realization that someday, soon, it will be finished.

7. Jesus called out with a loud voice, "Father, into your hands I commit my spirit." When he had said this, he breathed his last. (Luke 23:46)

Luke gives us Jesus' final words of lament amidst the cosmic upheaval of darkness and the torn curtain of the Temple. He wants us to know that it was a *loud* voice that Jesus cried out in. In fact, when the centurion who watched the Crucifixion heard the cry, he praised God and noted that surely Jesus was a righteous man. He had seen hundreds — perhaps thousands — of men die from crucifixion. Never had he seen someone die with a victorious shout. (I like to think that this man became a part of the early church. There is a strange statement in John 19:34-35 that could have only come from someone like him.)

This moment represents the end of the journey of lament for Jesus. Notice that the title "Father" has reappeared. They are completely one once more. Now Jesus, who had been uniquely gifted with the power to let go of His life (John 10:18), does just that, committing it to the hands of His Father.

Through the journey of lament, we discover that the end is really the beginning. When the struggle with the darkness is endured, a new hope is always waiting for us at the end of the road. For Job it was the statement, "My ears had heard of you, but now my eyes have seen you" (Job 42:5).

When the initial issues, the pleas for provision, are exhausted through lament, we learn that what we ask for in prayer is almost never what we really need. At the end, it is only "Father, into your hands I commit my spirit."

For Discussion

1. Read Psalm 22 together and then spend a few moments in silence.

2. Why is it significant that Jesus "gave up his spirit," that no one took His life from Him?

For Meditation

1. Reread the seven last words from the cross, but this time hear them as short, gasping phrases.

2. Meditate on the concept of Jesus' experience of hell on the cross as the hidden face of God.

38 | The Rending of God's Garment

With a loud cry, Jesus breathed his last.
The curtain of the temple was torn in two from top to bottom.
MARK 15:37-38

When Joseph's deceitful brothers brought back what was left of his special long-sleeved robe, soaked in the blood of a goat, poor Jacob, who had deceived so many others, was himself deceived. He came to the erroneous conclusion his sons hoped he would. He believed his precious Joseph had been torn to pieces by wild animals. Even before he wept, the first thing the old man did in response to his grief was to tear his robe (Genesis 37:34).

When the final messenger came to Job with the tragic news that a desert wind that blew from four directions at once had destroyed the house in which his children were celebrating one of their worrisome parties, their father got up from the ground and ripped the robe he was wearing (Job 1:20).

What little evidence there is points to the fact that the rending of the garment was a custom that went all the way back to ancient Mesopotamia. Together with the sprinkling of dust on the head and sometimes even the shaving of the head, the tearing of the robe was considered a sign of intense mourning. It is believed that originally these customs were a means for the living to identify with the dead. To ruin your robe in such a way and cover your face with dust was to adopt the appearance of your loved one who had died. It was a wordless way of saying what so many mourners, especially those who mourn for their own children have said: "I wish it could have been me instead."

At the precise moment of Jesus' death, the synoptic Gospels all tell us that the veil of the Temple was torn from top to bottom. In addition, Luke provides the detail that darkness covered the whole land (23:44). Even more remarkable, Matthew tells of an earthquake that split the rocks and broke open the tombs of many holy people. He goes on to say that these same people made their way into Jerusalem and appeared to many people after the resurrection of Jesus (Matthew 27:51-53).

The synoptic Gospels are painting a cosmic picture for us. The sun could not bring itself to shine down on such a heartbreaking scene. The earth itself seemingly could not bear the weight of what was happening, and so it shuddered. The impression is that in distant galaxies stars collapsed and the courses of planets were altered by it. The immensity of the moment, the nexus of the history of the universe, could not be overstated. Of all the impossible things we could imagine, this — the death of God — was the most impossible.

It is not possible to determine which veil the Gospels are referring to, since there were two inside the Temple. This is another example of one of those times when any of us, equipped with the facts, can make a guess that is just as good as a scholar's.

The first candidate was the veil that hung at the entrance to the Holy of Holies. According to Jewish tradition recorded in the Mishnah, it was one handbreadth thick, forty cubits long, and twenty wide. It was blue, purple, and scarlet. The historian Josephus, himself once a priest, said that it typified the universe (Exodus 26:31-35; Leviticus 16:2). The other possible candidate was the veil that was used to separate the sanctuary from the outer porch, or forecourt (Exodus 26:36-37).

If the second veil was the one that was torn, it would have made for a much more public sign, since everyone would have seen it. If it was the first veil, the one in front of the Holy of Holies, only a few privileged priests would have witnessed it.

Since none of the Gospels provide an interpretation as to what the rending of the Temple veil means, we are left once more with at least a couple of choices. The most popular interpretation is that the veil that was torn was the one in front of the Holy of Holies, signifying that now the way to God was open to all people, not just a single priest once a year on the Day of Atonement. The old system of sacrifice had come to an end since God had offered the perfect sacrifice of His own Son (Hebrews 10:5-14). The other major understanding sees the outer veil as the one that was torn, symbolizing the rending of the flesh of Jesus, and also a portent of the eventual destruction of the Temple in AD 70.

Behind both these interpretations is another more recent idea that has only been suggested by scholars in the past few decades. What if the rending of the veil of the Temple was God's own lamenting response to the death of His Son? Whether it was the outer or the inner veil that was torn, could it be that it was a sign that God Himself was mourning the crucifixion, that He was participating in the cosmic reaction to the impossibility of Jesus' death? As Job and Jacob and so many others had done before and are still doing today, was the Father responding to the worst news that any father can receive, that His child was dead? Amos speaks of such cosmic mourning:

> I will make the sun go down at noon
> and darken the earth in broad daylight.
> I will turn your religious feasts into mourning
> and all your singing into weeping.
> I will make all of you wear sackcloth
> and shave your heads.
> I will make that time like mourning for an only son
> and the end of it like a bitter day.
> (Amos 8:9-10; see also Zechariah 12:10)

The Bible does not say for certain that the torn curtain was an act of lament by the Father of Jesus, but we do know that lament, as we have seen time and time again, makes uniquely possible the opening of a way that did not exist before. Though we do not know which veil it was, we are certain that one of them was torn from top to bottom, irreparably destroyed. Though we cannot be sure of the reason for its being rent, we know for certain that the tearing of the garment was a sign of intense mourning. The most widely held interpretation of the rending of the veil of the Temple states that because a pair of powerful, invisible hands tore the thick curtain in two, a new way was open to us all — the possibility of direct communication with God. That the Father lamented the death of the Son is beyond question. That He tore His garment, the veil of the Temple in response, seems a fascinating and heartbreaking possibility.

Within each one of us lies a holy of holies, curtained with a veil. When God's spirit comes to inhabit this place, the image of our being a temple becomes complete. Someone has said that we never come to God, He comes to us. If that is true, He comes from His holy place to ours, making it holy. He comes across a bridge of tears, of our repentance and His joy. And perhaps He comes with a garment that has a tear in it, that matches the wounds of His own Son.

For Discussion

1. Are there any parallels in our culture to the rending of the garment?
2. Why do we lack such a dramatic expression of grief?

For Meditation

1. Is it possible to imagine the cosmic upheaval caused by the Crucifixion apart from Hollywood special effects? Have you ever experienced an earthquake?
2. Respond to the idea that each of us has inside us a holy of holies. Invite the Lord to come and inhabit that place.

39 | To Know Christ

I want to know Christ and the power of his resurrection and the fellowship of sharing in his sufferings, becoming like him in his death, and so, somehow, to attain to the resurrection from the dead. Not that I have already obtained all this, or have already been made perfect, but I press on to take hold of that for which Christ Jesus took hold of me.

PHILIPPIANS 3:10-12

Paul had been awaiting his trial in Rome for over two years. Initially, he had only been under house arrest and apparently enjoyed some degree of freedom, which he used for teaching and preaching. His work already had an impact, for Paul wryly states in the closing of his letter, "All the saints send you greetings, *especially those who belong to Caesar's household*" (Philippians 4:22, emphasis added).

But the mood seems to be shifting by the time he writes the letter to the Philippians. Perhaps his trial had already started, since he refers to his defense and hopes for acquittal (1:7,19-26; 2:23-24). That Paul is innocent is clear. Whether the demonical person judging his case will understand this is doubtful. His name was Nero.

Aside from all the legal controversies, aside from the persecution that is building against the church, aside from the very real prospect of a Roman execution by beheading, Paul is mindful of one simple truth as he nears the end of his journey — he is about to be "poured out"(Philippians 2:17). It has been said that the prospect of death marvelously focuses the mind. Paul's mind has but one focus: Christ.

He is nearing the end of the same journey as people like Job, David, and Jeremiah. Like each of their journeys, Paul's began with a burning desire for the "righteousness that comes from the law." In his former life as a Pharisee, righteousness was all that mattered. Now, at the end of the journey, all that has changed. His attention is fixed on the person of Jesus of Nazareth. In Him all of Paul's hopes reside, and so he wants only one thing from the journey: to know Christ, no matter what it costs.

All his years of ministry have taught Paul that the path to knowing Christ and His resurrection power is the path of lament: "the fellowship of sharing in his sufferings" (Philippians 3:10). If you could ask the apostle what lament is all about, he would simply answer, "It's about knowing Christ." That is everything. Nothing else matters, whether you are facing execution or just the prospect of another meaningless day — only the knowledge of Jesus Christ, gained through redemptively entering into His sufferings, can give perspective and meaning to life. "To live is Christ," Paul said to the Philippians (1:21).

Paul's life had been pouring out for years as he opened the door of the kingdom to anyone who would listen. Whether they lived in Caesar's house or a hovel, be they Athenian philosopher or slave girl, Paul was always ready to enter into their confusion and shine the light he had been given, making Jesus visible, believable, and beautiful so that the world could love Him more. He had wept with the churches. He had wept for the churches (2 Corinthians 2:4; Philippians 3:18; 2 Timothy 1:4). He had built a bridge of lament, made of his own tears. That bridge is always there. The door, though sometimes obscured by our pain and doubt, is always open. And waiting on the other side is the One who weeps our tears and promises someday to wipe them out altogether (Revelation 21:4). He is the incarnation of the *hesed* of the God who is moved by our tears.

It was Paul who recognized that the compassionate face of God had been unveiled in Jesus. "For God, who said, 'Let light shine out of darkness,' made his light shine in our hearts to give us the light of the knowledge of the glory of God in the face of Christ" (2 Corinthians 4:6). His is no longer a hidden face. It is always present on the journey of lament.

However, the journey is not over yet. Paul expresses the hope of it when he closes with the words, "But I press on" (Philippians 3:12). The call is to press on, to not let go, to never leave the dance floor until the music is over.

We are still on this journey, together. Don't give up. Keep reaching out to take hold of the One who is holding on to you, no matter how much it costs.

For Discussion

1. Compare the life journeys of Job and Paul. They both started with a preoccupation with Torah obedience. Where did they both conclude their journeys?

2. How is it that for Paul as well as thousands of Christians today, the prospect of suffering intensifies and strengthens faith?

For Meditation

1. Meditate on the implications of the statement, "For me to live *is* Christ," in light of the fallen nature of the world.

2. When Christ issued the call to Saul, who became Paul, He said to Ananias, "I will show him how much he must suffer for my name" (Acts 9:16). What effect did that suffering seem to have on Paul as he approached his execution?

40 | The End Must Always Be a Beginning

I am the Alpha and the Omega, the Beginning and the End.

REVELATION 21:6

Years ago, in a college history class, my professor made two enormous marks on the blackboard. One was an almost perfect circle. (*He has done this before,* I thought to myself.) The other was a straight line that stretched nearly the length of the wall.

"You have two choices," he solemnly said. "Linear or cyclical; you must decide how you will view history."

It seemed a reasonable enough proposition. Does the flow of history follow a straight path toward the future or does it constantly double back on itself in a continuous circle?

As I pondered the choices, it occurred to me that perhaps if you took the circle and placed it on top of the line you would have a better, perhaps more elegant solution to the problem. Clearly there are cycles in history, of war and peace, famine and prosperity, freedom and despotism. But these cycles do not negate the fact that the whole of history, that time itself, is moving in the direction of a great climax. As the circle rolls along the line, the point of the cycle that was the beginning becomes the end and, after another revolution, becomes the beginning once again.

We have spoken of lament as a journey—a journey with a beginning and an end. There is great hope, it seems to me, that the journey *is* taking us somewhere: from Torah obedience to praise, from isolation to communion, from begging for provision to the great satisfaction of Presence. But, given the model of the circle and the line, it seems to me that there is a cycle involved as well. We move from dark times to light and then back again, learning the same lessons over and over again. When we are in the darkness, knowing that the Light will inevitably return is a reason for hope. When we are in the light, an awareness that the darkness may certainly return becomes an occasion for savoring, for more deeply appreciating the Light (John 12:35-36).

> Weeping may remain for a night,
> but rejoicing comes in the morning. (Psalm 30:5)

We don't tend to see beautiful sunsets at the end of bad days. But the beauty of a sunset is all the more beautiful because we believe and trust and hope that another day is coming.

"La tristesse durera toujours"

If the psalmist is right and weeping lasts only for a night, then van Gogh must be wrong. The sadness cannot last forever. While Vincent could glory in the sunset — even paint it powerfully for you and me — it seems that finally, in the end, he was unable to see, even with his remarkable eye, that another new day was coming.

And if he was mistaken about tears, I believe he was wrong about the missing door he could not bring himself to paint. While it may sometimes be hidden from us, the truth is, it is not missing, ever. A way in always exists. And behind that door, which is sometimes so hard to find, Someone waits with His hand on the latch.

If, as you read these words, there are tears in your eyes, God is not far away, but unimaginably close — as close, or closer, than your own tears. If you are still looking for the way in, then here is your hope: the Way has become a person who is moved by those tears. If you have given up the hope of even looking for the door, if you feel you have come to the most bitter end, then this is precisely where you must start, for the end is always a beginning.

Notes

1. Richard Stengel, "Fly Till I Die," *Time*, April 22, 1996.
2. Ekkehard Schuster and Reinhold Boschert-Kimmig, *Hope Against Hope: Johann Baptist Metz and Elie Wiesel Speak Out on the Holocaust* (Mahwah, NJ: Paulist Press, 1999), 97.
3. Abraham Joshua Heschel, *Man Is Not Alone* (New York: Farrar, Straus, Giroux, 1951), 296.
4. Walter Brueggemann, *Awed to Heaven, Rooted to Earth: Prayers of Walter Brueggemann* (Minneapolis: Fortress Press, 2003), 87.

About the Author

Michael Card is an award-winning musician, author, and teacher. His many songs include "El Shaddai" and "Immanuel." He has written numerous books, including *A Violent Grace, The Parable of Joy, A Fragile Stone,* and *A Sacred Sorrow.* A graduate of Western Kentucky University with a bachelor's and a master's degree in biblical studies, Michael is currently at work on a PhD in classical literature. He lives in Tennessee with his wife and four children. For more information, please visit www.michaelcard.com.

MORE COMPELLING BOOKS TO BRING YOU CLOSER TO GOD.

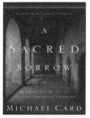

A Sacred Sorrow

Michael Card   1-57683-667-3

By investigating the lives of Job, David, Jeremiah, and Jesus, Michael Card shows how voicing our sincere yet humble dissatisfactions can be a cathartic completion of our worship and love of God.

A Sacred Sorrow Experience Guide

Michael Card   1-57683-668-1

With this Bible study, you and your small group can fully grasp the importance of voicing your heart's joys and pains to the Father. Go even deeper into the eye-opening message of *A Sacred Sorrow* and discover what's been missing in your prayers and worship.

The One True Thing

Howard Baker   1-57683-695-9

Deep within our hearts, we desire to make God the sole subject of our affection. But everyday life has a way of fragmenting our pursuit and realigning our priorities. Howard Baker presents a path to reclaiming our lives and time for Him, guiding us to seek, choose, and ultimately value our relationship with Him above all else.